**WINNER
PEACE**

WINNER PEACE

How to End Inner Conflict and Make Success Inevitable

RYAN CHRISTENSEN
with Joshua Lisec

All rights reserved. No part of this publication may be reproduced, distributed, or transmitted in any form or by any means, including photocopying, recording, or other electronic or mechanical methods, without the prior written permission of the publisher, except in the case of brief quotations embodied in critical reviews and certain other noncommercial uses permitted by copyright law.

This book is a work of nonfiction. The author has made every effort to ensure the accuracy of the information herein. However, the author and publisher assume no responsibility for errors, omissions, or damages caused by the use of the information contained herein.

Copyright © 2024 by Ryan Christensen

Publisher's Cataloging-in-Publication

Names: Christensen, Ryan (Ryan Wayne), author.
Title: Winner peace : how to end inner conflict and make success inevitable / Ryan Christensen.
Description: Austin, Texas : Requiem Hypnosis, [2024] | Includes bibliographical references.
Identifiers: ISBN: 979-8-9914095-0-6 (hardcover) | 979-8-9914095-1-3 (softcover) | 979-8-9914095-2-0 (ebook)
Subjects: LCSH: Peace of mind. | Success. | Self-perception. | Self-esteem. | Self-actualization (Psychology) | Thought and thinking. | Emotions. | LCGFT: Self-help publications.
Classification: LCC: BF637.P3 C47 2024 | DDC: 158.1--dc23

Contents

Preface: Is It Ever Going to End? 1
Introduction: There Is No Needle 3
   What Pain Demands: Cage or Treadmill 8
   How You Know This Book Works (And for You, Too).......12
Chapter 1: Why You Can't Control Your Mind..............15
   Your Four Minds 17
Chapter 2: Solving the Problem Where It Is 33
   How the Minds Think and Solve Problems 34
Chapter 3: Stop Coping and Start Curing 41
   Modalities That Don't Work (And Why)...................42
   On Pain Relief 51
Chapter 4: How Beliefs Control Everything 53
   How Not to Change Beliefs..............................60
Chapter 5: Rewrite the Past................................63
   Reframing without Lying................................65
   Specific Beliefs We All Want Changed 71
Chapter 6: You're Safe Now.................................75
Chapter 7: Make Your Emotions Work for You................79
   Your Five Survival Responses (And How to Hack Them) 83
   Unconscious Coercion: The Three Archetypes 85
Chapter 8: How to Feel Valuable...........................91
Chapter 9: What You Want Is Inevitable 101
Chapter 10: Now That Everything Has Changed 107
   Wants versus Needs: A New Perspective..................108
   The Games We Play......................................110
   The Next Step..117
Acknowledgments..119

PREFACE

IS IT EVER GOING TO END?

The exact moment I realized I needed to write this book came one hour, six minutes, and thirty-nine seconds into, of all things, an interview with Russell Brand.

Russell appeared on *Diary of a CEO* and shared the following at that opportune time stamp. I stopped what I was doing, paused the episode, rewound, and listened again. And again and again and again. Here's what Russell said that ultimately brought this book to you—and you to this book:

> I have to do quite a lot to not be crazy. I have to do the hot, the cold, the BJJ, the yoga. There's someone I worked with once who said, "Every day I get up, I meditate, I pray, I exercise, I do green juice, I do hot, I do cold, I attend a support group, and then I feel . . . OK. That's what I get to feel if I do all that. Then I don't feel like a lunatic vacillating wild lasso of mad vicissitude that could lash around anything in the search for connection."[1]

The show's host then asked Russell, in almost as many words, "Is it ever going to end? Will we be dealing with this our whole lives?"

---

1 - Steven Bartlett, "Russell Brand FINALLY Opens Up: Escaping a Lifetime of Anxiety, Addiction, and Finding Love!," June 29, 2023, in *The Diary of a CEO*, podcast, MP3 audio, 01:36:30, www.youtube.com/watch?v=EXUpMMde51E&t=3999s.

Russell replied. He went on and on about emotional wounds, internal strength, character qualities, and vulnerability. But he didn't answer the question.

I get it, though. The people I've worked with live that life. They've been working on their traumas, pains, and insecurities for years. They've tried everything. They've seen some results. But they are not "healed" in any meaningful or measurable way. They're coping as best they can. It's far better than it was, but they're still coping. And just barely, they feel OK at the end of it all. Not *better*. Not like a winner at all.

It's time to stop coping and start winning.

INTRODUCTION

THERE IS NO NEEDLE

It's almost impossible to find a needle in a haystack. You know what's even harder than trying to find a needle in a haystack? Trying to find a needle in a haystack when there is no needle in the haystack!

What if you thought there was something wrong with you, but the only thing that's ever been wrong was the situation you were in? What if it's not you? And what if it never was?

This might be the first time you've considered this. For so long, you've probably been feeling that something *was* wrong with you. Most men I meet through my line of work have been trying to "fix" themselves for years, driven by this pervasive feeling that you need to be different. Better. Or else you'll never get what you want.

Just look at you. I mean, *obviously* something's up. Have you struggled with procrastinating? Avoiding unpleasant, uncomfortable people, places, and things? Have you had these boom-and-bust cycles where you made progress, petered out, and fell back? Got stuck and couldn't seem to move forward in your finances or with your fitness? Or maybe you got stuck and stayed that way until it became your new normal, so now it doesn't even feel like you're stuck anymore. Life's OK, but if you're honest, you're getting maybe 20 percent of what you want out of it. Maybe pushing 40 percent on a good day. It's just to stay hungry. Not even to chase more. But *what if*, you know? What if.

Or perhaps you're on the complete opposite end of the dissatisfaction spectrum. Maybe you're constantly focused on your career or your business. It consumes so much of your time and attention that there's little left for anything else. You're constantly trying to optimize every aspect of your life to get the most out of each moment. Perhaps you've got a complex morning routine, designed to get you in just the right mindset to tackle the day. Do you constantly compare yourself to people more successful than you, using that pain to drive you forward? When will enough be enough? Can it? What will it feel like to finally make it? Is that even possible?

What about your social life? If you're in a new social setting where you don't know anybody, how does it usually play out? Do you arrive at the event and watch how the crowd is behaving to determine what you're supposed to do, hiding in a back corner until you figure that out? By your own admission, you probably aren't exactly the life of the party. You just want to adopt a persona that other people will find acceptable. This hasn't been easy.

And what about your romantic relationships? This is the one place where you cannot hide who you are for long; you can't hide your flaws, perceived flaws, or anything you don't like about yourself. You've probably felt like you've had to settle in some way, shape, or form—either with hot short-term things or with longer-term stability that brings dysfunction and disappointment. Whatever that is for you, you probably haven't been able to get what you need in your closest, most intimate relationships. You've taken what comes your way rather than gone out and gotten what you truly wanted. Maybe because you felt like you didn't deserve it.

Now let me ask you about something else—about when you've felt like you were at your worst. Depression. Despair. Darkness. How bad has all that been? How deep was the hole? How hard is it to get out?

For most men, it's fucking hard. But not because they don't try. It's because they try *everything*. Maybe you have, too. Therapy,

INTRODUCTION - THERE IS NO NEEDLE

coaching, exercise, retreats, breath work, energy healing, acupuncture, supplements, biohacking, medication, maybe even psychedelics. You've already been working your ass off to address your well-being on a regular basis. Get out of that hole. Meditate and journal your way out. Get out with a cold plunge. Spend hours at the gym. Go on retreats. Anything and every other thing to manage your emotional state—to stay those feelings of shame, guilt, insecurity, and doubt. Man, they're a bitch.

And yet she doesn't go away, does she? No matter what you do, it doesn't feel like enough.

Now let me ask you another question.

What if that's a good thing?

What if there isn't anything wrong with you? What if you were simply forced into situations where there were no ways to win, and you did the best you could?

What if you're looking for a needle in a haystack—the solution to your problems, the answer to finally fix yourself, the way to be better and feel better—but there is no needle?

But, Ryan, there has *to be a needle! There has to be a way to get better and feel different—because I sure* don't *feel OK. This pain is* real.

If that's you, I do not blame you one bit. The pain inside feels real, yes. All emotions, pain included, have two aspects: First, there's a *physiological* response in the body, preparing you for action. Anger, for example, readies you for a fight. Then there's the *mental* aspect of an emotion. We interpret feelings like fear, sadness, and anger as pain, but that's not what those signals mean.

This is where things get weird. You know that physiological response to the feeling? Any feeling? Like anger, where you feel it, *but you feel it*—it's an actual physical experience. Breathing shallows, heart beats faster, face gets red. All that. It means your body is doing exactly what it's supposed to be doing. Think about that: *When you feel overcome by an emotion, it means your body is working.* When your body experiences fight, flight, freeze, and so on—wherever and whenever—nothing is wrong with your body's processes. Because if there is a threat, you *should* be fighting, fleeing, or freezing! Understand that your body is trying to help you survive. The "pain" is telling us what needs to change and where. And this is the problem—*we are not the problem.* We don't need to look *inside* ourselves for a problem that's *outside* ourselves. You're not supposed to go into fight, flight, or freeze *against or in response to yourself.* That's just silly. You are not your own self-threat. That is not a thing. You are *not* the problem.

Let's take it further.

Negative emotions (the pain of guilt, shame, anxiety, doubt, etc.) are your mind asking you to help solve a problem out in the world, not within you (although that's where you feel the emotions because you are, in fact, a person, so where else *could* you feel your feelings?).

Take anger, for example: *There's a problem to fix, and I need* force *to solve it.* That's when you experience that emotional state: anger. Now take another one: *There's something dangerous here, right now, and I need to get away.* That's fear. Your mind is asking for help; these requests for help are emotions.

Starting to make sense?

Good.

Can you see how dangerous it is to call these cries for help "pain"? Why equating negative feelings with *who you are as a person* is the exact opposite message those emotions are trying to send?

Yeah. That's a little screwed up. I might be the first person to tell you this. I'm sorry it took this long, but I'm glad you came.

Let's continue our line of thinking. All feelings, even and especially negative ones, are actually helpful signals. Requests for help. *There is a problem here, and I need you to get resources to solve it.* What happens when you ignore that emotion, though? Stuff it? Resist it? Attend talk therapy and eat mushrooms to distract yourself from it?

INTRODUCTION - THERE IS NO NEEDLE

Avoidance of a negative yet purposeful emotion tells your mind that you can't solve the problem. Disempowering. Ouch. You're basically saying to yourself, *I don't know how to deal with this situation. I don't know how to survive it* So then it goes from an acute concern to a chronic concern. This is the ramification: Not only do you not know how to handle this situation, you're soon convinced you can't handle any similar situations. This makes you mentally and emotionally brittle, very quickly.

It can get worse. The more severe the negative emotion, the more intolerable the situation, the more desperate you are to get out and get free, the greater the impact that experience has on how much your mind wants to protect you—*from yourself.* And so your unconscious mind now has to protect you from yourself. When we frame negative emotions as pain, we're telling the survival-oriented part of our mind—the part that's there to keep us breathing and doesn't care whether or not we're happy—to treat our emotional state as *a threat to our physical survival.*

If you've been in significant, persistent negative emotional states, ultimately resulting in falsely equating *how you feel with who you are as a person*, that's like being in significant physical pain. It's like getting stabbed or being attacked by a dog. It triggers the same survival mechanisms, all because we defined painful emotion as . . . well, pain. Not good. And yet this is what the entire $10 billion self-help industry teaches us to do. You're told that *you* need help when you are *not* the problem. The difficulty or conflict came from how you acted or reacted to external environmental factors. You are not the problem. The problem is the problem. There is no needle.

Maybe there's no haystack either.

This is quite a way to begin a book, isn't it?

If we're going to feel better, to feel OK again, to feel like and become a champion in *all* areas of life, we've got to know what is real and what is an illusion and why—and what to do about it.

What Pain Demands: Cage or Treadmill

Most men, dealing with what they perceive to be deep pain compounded over the years—with the ramification being the incorrect belief that the problem is from within, that *they* are the problem—will run to the cage or hop on the treadmill.

If you can escape inner turmoil by changing your environment or circumstances, you might choose to flee as a survival strategy. This is the treadmill. You will feel constant pressure to keep succeeding in bigger and better ways. You'll feel like you're not good enough and try to prove that feeling wrong. It doesn't work, doesn't matter, keep doing it. Here's what I mean; you might relate: You're constantly grinding toward your goals, consuming all your time and energy. Eventually you reach your goals and feel good for a little while, then it's back to feeling empty. So you set a bigger, more impressive goal to chase after. The last one wasn't enough, and this one won't be either. Oh well. Keep running.

Then there's the cage, where you're unsafe to even try going big because you might fail. So you self-entrap your life. Just turtle up and take it. This keeps you in a place where everything is easy to do. Life is OK, but you're stuck in mediocrity. The problem is that everything that makes life worth living is outside the cage.

Recall that when we reframe emotions as bad pain and not as good signals (which they are), we reassign the actual problem (that thing or situation outside ourselves) to who we are as people, as men. Which is not correct. But it's so typical. It's easy to do. It's normal. So normal that you're probably wondering if there's any way *I* could possibly be correct! But consider what treating pain as bad, not good, does: *You have to run from yourself or hide from yourself.* The former is the treadmill; the latter is the cage. The existential threat isn't reality itself; it's your emotional response to it. Too much emotional pain, and you might feel like you want to die. It's awful. And yet that is exactly what happens when you train your subconscious mind not to trust your conscious mind. It can't let you change your unconscious beliefs because all the changes you want to make are considered dangerous. This makes changing those beliefs yourself basically impossible.

Welcome to the cage.

Here in the cage, the lights are on and the bills are paid, but life feels empty. You have big dreams that stay that way. You never go after what you want and simply settle for what comes your way . . . especially romantically.

Setting Our Own Traps

What makes the treadmill and the cage traps is that they feel productive—or at least not *unproductive*. You've probably heard that living organisms, including people, move away from pain and toward pleasure. This is somewhat descriptive but is mistaken as *prescriptive*. It's terrible advice, actually. And yet that seems like a pretty good thing to do, no? Avoid what feels bad; do what feels good?

The problem with this dichotomy is that there is no space reserved for neutrality. There's no space for a moment when you're not moving *toward* or *away*. When you're OK. When you just "are".

What this means if you're a high-performing treadmiller is that there is never any state where you can just be still. Just be. You're either running from your pain or you're running toward pleasure. You're never stopping, never slowing down, never pausing to rest. You are stuck in survival mode; everything is an emergency all the time. There's always this impulse to "do something" because every time you stop moving, all the thoughts about how terrible and fake and weak and disappointing you really are (*if they only knew!*) rear their ugly heads. You get stuck in little doom loops, having to cope with an army of insecurities. Better to stay busy.

Now if you're in the cage, you'll find yourself lulling your pain into silence via distractions and their fake dopamine. Or worse, with addictions. And yet you're safe in that fine little prison because there is so much *pleasure*. But it's not real. It's not the thrill of victory or the meaning of achievement. Because that all takes risk, which is dangerous. Too risky to try because you might fail. *You're not the kind of person who can handle failure,* the mind says. So back into the cage it is, and here we will stay!

But time in the comfort cage soon begins to numb the feel-goods. So you need feel-betters. More of them. Way more. And that is how people become alcoholics. And I don't just mean alcoholics. (Both cold plunges and cocaine spike your dopamine by a factor of 2.7. Interesting.)

Either way, treadmill or cage, life in the traps means you're never at neutral. Never at rest. And that's tricky because chasing (or basking in) pleasure means running or hiding from the pain—which is there for a good reason in the first place, remember? To help you. To inform you that an external situation outside yourself requires your attention. To wave red flags and light you up with signals to capture your full awareness so that you'll solve that problem out there.

No more traps. No more extremes.

This book will help you. Help you find neutral and feel it. All of it. Where you don't have to chase pleasure because you can release the pain—by knowing it for what it is, not just realizing what it does. Because rational understanding is not enough to make you a champion. I want you to *experience* it. To *be* it.

And so with this book, we will help you get out of the cage and off the treadmill—and stay out and stay off. We're going to reframe all pain, hurt, and even trauma as requests for help that you will now be able to respond to appropriately in the moment and without anxiety prior to or perpetual fear after.

We will bring to an end your shame and fear and the feeling that you need to prove yourself all the time. And therefore . . . an end to working on yourself all the time. We'll bring you to a place where your deepest beliefs are that there's nothing wrong with you, where there's nothing left to heal, where you're good enough as you are to deserve whatever you choose, and that it's inevitable that you'll get everything you want and need in life.

There's more. Reading and applying this book will help you do the following:

- Feel at peace, centered, and in control—all as your baseline emotional state.
- Stop spending hours on complex routines to manage your feelings.
- Have a full, well-rounded life without feeling like you're sacrificing your mission or your purpose.
- Feel unshakeable confidence in yourself, certainty that you're good enough, with no need to prove it to anyone—not even yourself anymore.
- Stop asking if you deserve things and simply focus on getting them.

This approach works. It's different from anything you've done before. Let me introduce you to some of my past clients who can help prove it to you.

How You Know This Book Works (And for You, Too)

Ellian struggled with severe abandonment issues throughout her life and had difficulty advancing her business despite knowing what was necessary. Before seeking my help, she had spent more than $70,000 trying to overcome these challenges. Shortly after our first session, Ellian got engaged to her boyfriend and was able to fully utilize her talents in her business.

Eric suffered from a chronic medical condition that debilitated him, often leaving him bedridden for weeks and unable to engage in daily activities. After working with me, he reached a point where he no longer felt the need to justify his existence and could easily manage his thoughts throughout the day. He became much more social and secured a new job that doubled his salary within weeks.

Deron battled suicidal thoughts and self-medicated with marijuana and alcohol. He would make progress toward his goals but frequently got sidetracked by life's pressures and sought escape through substances. Now he consistently adheres to his gym routine and diet and has embarked on his dream career as a stand-up comedian.

Vic, an older gentleman, struggled with dating after his divorce, feeling inadequate despite being in shape and financially stable. After our sessions, he not only gained the confidence to approach women he was interested in, he also became so confident that women began approaching him in bars and restaurants.

Natalie had been dealing with drug addictions and suicidal thoughts for decades, living for others and trapped in a cycle of overthinking. Today she enjoys a peaceful mind, prioritizes her needs, and pursues her dreams.

I would like for you to be next.

That said, there is one scenario in which I've seen the methods in this book fail—when there is *significant* self-hatred and self-loathing. This isn't merely disliking yourself; it's an intense, continuous self-punishment due to not meeting certain ego demands. It reflects a deep-seated (false) belief that you are the problem.

If you are open to questioning the belief that something is fundamentally wrong with you, then this approach can work for you.

Now consider the final alternative to this book: *If everything else you've tried was going to work, wouldn't it have by now? How much longer do you want to spend on ineffective solutions? Do you want to merely* cope *with your problems indefinitely, or do you want to be free from pain, fear, insecurity, and doubt—forever?*

To achieve freedom from pain you don't need, you must follow a specific sequence—the sequence we are about to begin.

Freedom is a path taken one step at a time—a linear, progressive journey.

Embark on this journey with me.

Off the treadmill and out of the cage—here we go!

CHAPTER 1

WHY YOU CAN'T CONTROL YOUR MIND

There's something you should know about me. I spent twenty-three years working in the intelligence community. Of that, I spent five years in the Marine Corps as a Russian linguist, another six years in the Air National Guard working intel for F-16s and F-22 Raptors, then the rest on Predator drones and U-2 surveillance planes. While I was in the guard, I lived and worked in Washington, DC as a contractor for counterterrorism and counterproliferation operations. My objective was to keep bad hombres from getting nuclear weapons, ballistic missiles, and chemical weapons. As far as I can tell, I was successful.

And yet I have Asperger's syndrome. It is extremely difficult to navigate human beings while having Asperger's. So to survive "out there" in the world where those other humans are, I had to adapt to a world not made for people like me. I had to reverse engineer "normal," neurotypical people's belief systems, attitudes, and value sets to find my way in their world—and in mine. I wasn't able to rely on my instincts to do it for me. The process of learning through observation that everybody does, using mirror neurons to match and mimic what a human is supposed to do or say in a given situation . . . well, I can't do. I had to brute-force calculate how to think and talk and write like a human. It was weird.

It's also what first fascinated me with the human mind, how it operates, and why it can work against us. Or seems to, at least. The unconscious mind is a black box—one I like to open up and ask, *Show me how you work.* Decoding the unconscious mind in particular is helpful in the hypnotic suggestion work I do as Ryan the Hypnotist (www.ryanthehypnotist.com). That said, this is not exactly a book about hypnosis. Hypnotic suggestions are a tool to complete a process, but the process is more important. You do not need to understand hypnosis or have had a hypnosis session, nor listened to a recording before, for this material to benefit you.

Ryan, what the hell does any of this have to do with getting off the treadmill or getting out of the cage?

Because you need to know how your mind *works*. If you're going to solve a problem, you have to solve the problem where it is. If you break your leg, going on a diet won't help you.

In the West, we have a fetish for conscious, decisive action, so we tend to pursue only those solutions that are obviously rational. What if the problem is not located in the conscious, rational mind?

There is another place where the problems can be coming from that we can access and play with: the black box of the unconscious mind where emotions and feelings and instincts and urges rule all. Otherwise, to deploy rational solutions to irrational problems, we would be dealing with the *output* of the emotional mind rather than *reaching into* it, specifically the unconscious mind. That will cause us to continue equating emotional signals as pain, which we've established before that they are not.

And yet again the pain feels real. *Can we fix a feeling?* Ha! No. Not possible. A rational solution to an emotional concern—you see the problem. *You can't rationally work your way through an emotional process.*

What do we do instead? Well, we don't run through the process rationally, but it helps to *understand* the process. This is meta. It's worth knowing, and here's why:

If we can accept that emotional beliefs are true from an emotional perspective, not a logical one, then we can set about to work through altering those beliefs, including the felt belief that a perceived negative emotion is pain.

Because just telling you, "Oh, that pain isn't really pain; that trauma isn't real. Depression and anxiety and crippling self-doubt and a palpable sense of worthlessness . . . they're all a fake illusion." Yeah, sure, buddy. Claiming that or even accepting it doesn't relieve the feelings of pain or trauma or depression or anxiety or self-doubt or worthlessness. In fact, the mere logical acceptance of my thesis *probably makes it worse* because it might feel like you are denying the existence of something that feels real *and* you were supposed to feel better already. This book would truly suck if this were as far as we got.

It's not.

We continue.

Up next, the meta process of how your mind actually works, why you can't control it, and why that's OK.

Your Four Minds

There is not one perfect set of tools to solve every problem in life. Different levels of the mind exist to solve different problems and achieve different goals. I'll explain shortly.

But first, let me tell you about a guy named Barry Ritholtz. He was a Wall Street guy, running hedge funds and whatnot. The details and background aren't really that important. During the housing crisis of 2008 and 2009, Ritholtz warned that the value and risk models Wall Street firms were using for collateralized debt obligations were broken. And he dropped this quote that has stuck with me ever since I first heard it:

All models are wrong. Some models are useful.

What this means is that any given model is an abstraction, a map of reality. It's not reality itself. The map is not the terrain. Because it's an abstraction, because it's a map of a representation of reality, it's going to be *wrong* by default.

But maps are useful to get you from point A to point B—as long as you're using the right map for the journey. The map I use to make it to the local Starbucks is not the same map I should be using to drive from Austin, Texas, to Wichita, Kansas. That same map is a map I should not be using to plot my flight from Austin to Dubai. And that map is not one I should be using to call in artillery on a position on the battlefield in war. Different kinds of maps, different levels of specificity, different ways of measuring the relationship between two points in space. Each for a different purpose.

When solving problems, we need to use the right model with specificity that will actually be useful. The model that hypnotists use of *conscious mind* and *unconscious mind* is superior to the psychologist's model that *consciousness is everything*, where consciousness is the passive receiver of all this information coming in from day-to-day life. From that perspective, you have to deal with everything on a conscious level, but hypnotists understand that there are *at least* two minds, the conscious and the unconscious, and that you can work with the unconscious mind to alter your conscious life—that is, your thoughts, attitudes, and overall sense of mental, emotional, and spiritual well-being. This is what I want for you. This is why you are here.

CHAPTER 1 - WHY YOU CAN'T CONTROL YOUR MIND

That said, the hypnotic model of conscious versus unconscious is incomplete. For example, it is not sufficient to help someone with bipolar disorder. We need a more specific, more useful model of the mind that takes into account neurotransmitters and the function of various brain regions in order to handle that diagnosis and improve the patient's quality of life.

In my private practice with hypnosis clients, I have expanded the standard hypnotic model of conscious versus unconscious into the four levels of mind. The way I teach my clients about this is usually through conversation—through spontaneous Q&A. Here's what I mean.

When clients have come to me feeling stuck and expressing complaints such as . . .

- "I'm not getting what I want."
- "What if that's not what I want?"
- "What if I want something different?"
- "Why do I feel like I'm not in control of myself?"

. . . I will ask them this question:

What part of you is you?

Not a simple question. Because there are *four* different parts of the mind—that is, four minds:

1. The *conscious* mind
2. The *rational* mind
3. The *emotional* mind
4. The *instinctive* mind

Then you've got your brain's *neurochemistry*, which is distinct from yet interdependent on those others, so it can crank aspects of those different minds up and down. Meaning it's possible to increase or decrease the expression and processing of each of the four minds by changing up your neurochemistry.

In addition to our neurochemistry, we have our *physical* bodies, obviously meaning the meat suit we're running around in. If you're thinking about somatic work, you've also got an *emotional* body on top of (alongside? within?) that. And if you want to get woo-woo, you've got an *energetic* body or perhaps an *astral* body or otherwise a *soul* (if you're religious). So that's ten different pieces of you, at least!

So again I ask: *What part of you is you?*

Well, it's going to be the sum total of all that is what you as an individual are, won't it? But when most people talk about *I*, especially here in the Western world where you're probably reading this, they're talking about it mostly from the perspective of "I equals consciousness," or "I am my consciousness," which means that the rest of them—all that is *not* the conscious mind—is therefore *not* them. And that's, uh, odd. And problematic, for a few different reasons.

First of all, when people feel like they're not in control of themselves, what they're saying is that they don't have *conscious* control of themselves, or their self is not obeying what they consciously want, and it's setting them up for a war with the self. Rational consciousness is the part of themselves that they can understand and appreciate, but anything else is not considered OK. *LOL, what?* Yeah, exactly. It's like those nine-plus other parts are rebellious, or "not me" in some way. *LOL, what?*, indeed.

Consider the popular self-help cliche about letting go of that which no longer serves you. If you don't understand what those other aspects of "your self" are doing for you, how do you know what is serving you, what is not, what part of you it serves, and why? Because your emotional mind and your instinctive mind can have different needs and priorities than your rational mind and your consciousness. Think of the ego as the identity that is created by the conscious mind and the rational mind working together. Often what happens is that the

CHAPTER 1 - WHY YOU CAN'T CONTROL YOUR MIND

ego is built when people don't like who they are. They don't like who they *feel* they are, rather. They perceive they are not good enough, for example. So they try to create a different *me* or a different self that is more acceptable by some external standard. And that's where many problems start—namely, those traps called the treadmill and the cage. They want to be this other self, but they're chained to the totality of what they are—yet that is not what they want to be, or at least they don't feel like they should be. Every moment you are failing to be the person your ego insists you must be, you are SOL.

What then must we do? *Expand your sense of self.* Expand the definition of who you are to encompass all those different aspects of you, not just consciousness, but also your rational mind, your emotional mind, your instinct mind, your neurochemistry, your physical body, your emotional body, your energetic or astral body, your soul. The whole thing together is one coherent self, one *you*.

There's more. Understand that consciousness is not a single entity, as it has two specific roles to play in the life of every human being:

1. Act as CEO—that is, forward planner
2. Act as witness—that is, observer to everything

If you sit there and think about this, what happens when you *sit there and think about this*? You throw the question into your unconscious mind. You sit there and wait for an answer to appear. Things are happening, and consciousness doesn't seem to be doing a lot to influence that process. It's waiting for the answers, waiting for the rest of you to do what it needs to do.

One thing that happens with my clients, having come to understand the totality of *self*, is that they become less egotistical. Because once you make the totality of what you are acceptable—good, worthy, not broken, not flawed, integral, and inherently important—it's easier to let go of that conscious ego identity you've created because you can finally accept who you are, what you are, all that you are.

Ultimately, that's where you want to get to—a place of integration where all those different parts of you are working together in harmony, on the same team, in the same direction, working the same plans, playing the same game. Yes, consciousness exists to set the direction, to be the CEO and to be the witness. But it's in *charge*, not in *control*. It can't force the rest of you to obey. Trying to do so leads to a life of misery. The best we can do is *understand* the four minds and what, specifically, they do for you. There's even more there to learn, so let's zoom in on the four-mind map to see what it can offer us.

Four Minds, Four Functions

The brain is structured in three different layers: the instinctive lizard brain, the limbic system, and then the cortex, the wrinkly part on the outside where all of our higher functions are.

The way I look at it is this: Your *instinctive* mind is designed to keep you breathing, to keep you alive. It's made to deal with problems of physical survival. Food, shelter, base issues.

Every living being with a brain has an instinctive mind. But at a certain level of complexity, that part of the brain is unable to solve the problems it's faced with. Lizards have an instinctive mind, but they don't have an emotional mind; they're limited in the way they can move through the world. It's much more primitive than, say, a horse, giraffe, zebra, lion, tiger, or bear.

The *emotional* mind evolved to solve problems of coordination between different beings. Horses are incredibly emotional creatures. Cats are emotional creatures. Dogs are emotional creatures. Lions and tigers and so on all experience and display emotion. All those creatures are able to coordinate within their species and are sometimes even able to coordinate between species. Because of emotion.

CHAPTER 1 - WHY YOU CAN'T CONTROL YOUR MIND

So we can see the emotional mind as the part of the mind that was designed to solve the problem of *How do I interact with and coordinate with other beings?* And that's where the trickiness comes in, because the coordination between beings is dependent on shared belief sets.

The emotional mind is heavily concerned with what things *mean* rather than with what they *are*. Best-selling author and hypnotist Scott Adams has famously predicted that there is no way we can let artificial intelligence do its own thing; if it did, it would break society because it would reveal all the lies that we base society on. He's right. Every society, every group interaction, is based on shared beliefs, shared understandings of the world. And fundamentally, they are *all* arbitrary, but that's what the emotional mind was designed for—to figure out what things mean in a group context among individuals of the same and sometimes other species so that everyone involved can coordinate action.

However, the *rational* mind was designed to figure out how things work in the real world. How to work with objective reality, how to figure out what things are. Recall that the emotional mind is concerned with meaning. The rational, logical mind is concerned about things, about objects, about how they work, about their principles, about those things that are objectively verifiable. You know, those things that are true whether you want them to be or not. Gravity doesn't care how you feel about it. And that is what allows us to create rockets and bridges and agriculture. It's the part of our mind that is trying to figure out how things work.

The difference between the rational and the emotional mind is often referred to as left brain versus right brain. There are more than two brains, understand, but this popular map of the mind is generally helpful for understanding how humans think.

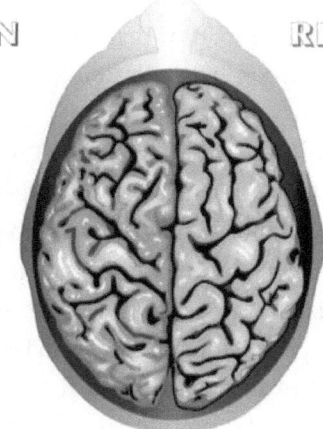

LEFT BRAIN
Logic
Reason
Objective
Verbal
Self-Orientated
Categorical
Detail focused
Mimicry
Purposefulness

RIGHT BRAIN
Intuition
Emotions
Subjective
Visual
Group-Orientated
Relational
Whole Picture focused
Creativity
Playfulness

This is not just for humans, by the way. Any tool-using being has that same capability. Monkeys, for example, use tools. Elephants play. And so on.

We've already introduced consciousness, with its two separate functions, roles, and problem-solving purposes. First, it's the part of us that is witnessing or watching the movie of our lives play out. It's the observer. It also the ultimate decider. The one to set the path, point the direction, and so on. It's the mind concerned with the future, with what should be, what ought to be, what we want to be.

There are four different parts of the mind that have four separate functions and are designed to solve four completely different types of problems. This is important because we know from neuroscience that different parts of our brains are *working independently*. They're not coordinating with one another.

When the Minds Disagree with Themselves

Ever heard of the Stroop test?

This beautiful little experiment was first used in university research. You get a volunteer, sit them in a chair, and show them words on a screen. The words are a particular color. You're supposed to press the button that corresponds to the color of the letters. So if the word is *gorilla*, and the color of the letters is green, you press the green button. If it's *house*, and the color of the letters is red, you press the red button. But if the word is *white* and the color of the letters is blue, now you've got a problem because the part of your brain that processes symbols says the correct answer is white because that's what that word means. The part of your brain that processes colors says the color of the letters is red, so the answer is red. Now you have two correct answers coming from two different parts of your mind.

It gets better (worse).

There's a third part of your mind that has to step in and decide which of those two correct answers is the most useful for dealing with the question being asked. There's a measurable delay when we see that word—when we've got a word that is a color but the name of that color does not match the color of the letters. Now if the word is *red* and the letters are red, there's no delay because those two answers are the same. There's no need to deconflict or deconstruct because both minds are coming up with the same answer.

This is fascinating because it means there are multiple kinds of truth—to your mind. Because "white" being the color is the correct answer from the symbolic perspective. "Red" is the correct answer from the perspective of the color of the letters, the physical color they are. Two correct answers that are completely different. Let me say that again. *Two correct answers that are completely different.*

This means your brain is analyzing the world and all the data in it from multiple perspectives simultaneously and coming up with answers independently. And those answers, even if both of them are correct, can differ.

That's where another part of your mind has to get involved and resolve that conflict in some way, shape, or form. This is where we run into trouble, but let me finish the story first.

A hypnosis experiment was conducted using the Stroop test. They got a bunch of volunteers together—people who were highly hypnotizable, and people who were not hypnotizable or were low on the hypnotizability scale—and ran them through a hypnotic induction, giving them the same suggestion, which was basically, "In a few days, you will go through an experiment where you're shown a series of meaningless symbols on a screen that are a particular color. Just press the button that corresponds to the color that you see on the screen." The researchers noticed something interesting when they ran the volunteers through the exam. The people who were not hypnotizable had that Stroop effect. They had that measurable delay when the word and the color conflicted—when the word was *white* and the color of the letters was red, or when the word was *red* and the color of letters was blue.

But the people who were highly hypnotizable showed no delay. Let me say that again. *The people who were highly hypnotizable had no delay.* There was no conflict because the suggestion was that those were meaningless symbols, which means whatever answer the symbolic part of your brain came up with was irrelevant because they were meaningless symbols. The only thing that mattered was the color they saw. They just pressed the button. There was no measurable delay, no Stroop effect. There was no conflict because their mind was looking at only one particular perspective.

We've built up to this: *We can use hypnosis to teach the mind how to process the world in a different way.* Or the "minds" how to process the world, to put it another way for the context of this chapter. We can teach you to listen to one source or another. We can teach you to favor

CHAPTER 1 - WHY YOU CAN'T CONTROL YOUR MIND

one thought or another. We can teach you how to coordinate better, internally.

Why is this important for making you feel like and actually *be* a champion in all areas of your life?

First, most people are experiencing a conflict between what they know should be and what they feel. What should be happening versus what is happening. What they know rationally and logically versus what they feel on an emotional level. And everybody thinks that one of those two things has to be wrong. I don't think that's true. Because the emotional mind and the rational mind are processing the world simultaneously but independently. They're coming up with answers independently. They're not talking to each other. But the answer that your rational mind provides is the correct answer from the rational perspective. The emotional response you get, the feeling you feel, is the correct answer *based on how the emotional mind is processing the world*.

So you don't have one right answer and one wrong answer. Most of the time, you're trying to figure out which answer is correct. But the reality is that you have two correct answers that are different because they're using different tools to analyze the same set of data.

An example is this idea of the difference between the median and the average. The *average* is when you sum up everything in a series and divide it by the number of things in the series; that number is the average of that series of numbers. The *median* is when you rank them all from top to bottom, from highest to lowest, and the median is the one in the middle. So if there are twenty of them, then number ten is the median. Let's say you've got 1,000 people, and of those thousand people, 999 people earn $0, but one guy makes $1 million. The average of that series is a thousand bucks. But the median is zero; guy number 500 in that series is making $0. In fact, everybody except that one guy is making $0. Is the correct answer $1,000, or is the correct answer $0? Again, they're both right based on the tools you're using to analyze the data. The same data can be looked at with two different sets of tools and come up with two completely different answers, both of which are correct based on the tool being used to analyze the world.

Everyone's trying to find the right answer, but there's more than one right answer depending on how you're processing the world.

The emotional conclusion you have about yourself is correct from an emotional perspective. The rational, logical conclusion you have about yourself is correct from a rational, logical perspective.

The trick is to understand why each of those is coming up with the different answers they are. Nobody asks, "Why do I feel this way?" Nobody gives that any credence, especially here in the West. We are so focused on rationality being the tool to navigate the world. And it's not. Rationality exists to solve a particular problem, and interacting with other people is not that freakin' problem. We're using the wrong tool. Emotions are what solve that. Again, that's what the emotional mind is for—solving interactions between people, *including your relationship with yourself.* This is crucial to effective change work. You are a person, too. And just like any one person, you have feelings about that individual—that you that is you, that is *all* of you.

I like to think of the four levels of mind as sources of four different kinds of truth. Consciousness is the arbiter or the intermediary that decides between and among them. We can't decide on an unconscious level, so we need consciousness to step in and do it for us. Your instinctive mind is like your worker drones; these are the ones on the loading dock and the ones in the accounting department. You can look at the emotional mind as middle management, the rational mind as upper management, and the consciousness as the CEO. What happens when the workers can't figure out what to do? They ask the emotional mind; they ask their bosses. The middle management types are supposed to get them what they need. If they can't, they ask senior management. If senior management can't get it, they ask the CEO.

CHAPTER 1 - WHY YOU CAN'T CONTROL YOUR MIND

Every single conflict between your rational and your emotional mind has to be resolved by the CEO. Management can't agree, so they have to go up to the big guy for a decision. But that's where suffering comes from—your consciousness gets bombarded by all these thoughts and feelings because your unconscious mind has no way to solve the conflict on its own. It has two correct answers and is incapable of deciding between them, so it has to ask somebody else for help. That's why it comes up into conscious awareness. And that's why it feels right to select conscious tools to work on these apparently conscious problems in life.

But because you have four different tools to analyze the world, you're coming up with four different kinds of answers, all of which are correct on their own level. Consider these as like four different compasses guiding us through life. The compass for the instinctive mind is pleasure and pain. If it feels good, do it. If it doesn't feel good, don't do it. If it's painful, avoid it. The good stuff feels pleasurable—that's the signal from the instinctive mind that says to go do that. Pain is the signal that says not to do that and cautions you about a problem.

The emotional mind, because it's concerned with meaning, is either good or bad, right or wrong. *Does this feel right? Then do it. Does this feel wrong? Then don't do it. Is this good? Yes. Is this bad? No.* But that's based on meaning, which we'll get to a little bit later. Good and bad are different from pleasure and pain—they're different signals that mean different things.

The rational mind is concerned with true and not true, factual and not factual. It's concerned with objective, verifiable reality and how things work. Gravity has an acceleration of 9.8 meters per second squared toward the center of the earth. If you said 7.2 meters per second, that's wrong. That's not true. The rational mind is concerned with facts and factual accuracy.

Consciousness, on the other hand, is concerned with want and don't want, or should and should not. It's taking all the inputs from the unconscious mind and saying, *Based on this input, I choose X. Based on this input, I choose to go down this path.* It's concerned with where we should go and what we should do based on what we want or what we've chosen.

Four different compasses, each designed to solve a different problem. We want all those compasses pointing in the same direction. *It should feel pleasurable, be a good thing, be true, and be something you want.*

Understanding *how* that works is a giant step of progress toward *making it work for you.*

You can look at it as a matrix between the thing we do and the reason we do it. You can do the right thing or the wrong thing for the right reason or the wrong reason. Doing the wrong thing for the wrong reason is always a bad idea—don't do that. Doing the wrong thing for the right reason is not good but is better than doing the wrong thing for the wrong reason. Doing the right thing for the wrong reason is also not a great idea. Ideally, we should try to do the right thing for the right reason.

We want to do the right thing for the right reason, rather than the right thing for the wrong reason, so that we do it the right way. If you're doing it for the wrong reason, your motivations and what you're trying to accomplish will be different—incorrect. You will go about it the wrong way.

A good example is the white savior complex—going to Africa to teach locals math, with the self-talk being, *I'm going to save the world. I'm going to show these backward people how things should be done.* You're trying to do the right thing, which is to help them live their lives in a better way, but you're doing it for the wrong reasons—because you're egotistical or you can't stand their suffering. So you end up doing it the wrong way. You don't help them the way they need or are asking to be helped. You help them the way you want to help them.

CHAPTER 1 - WHY YOU CAN'T CONTROL YOUR MIND

Doing the right thing for the wrong reason always ends badly because you do it the wrong way.

It's also important to distinguish between wants and needs. Wants are conscious things, and needs are unconscious things. Needs are more important. Put another way . . .

The priorities of the unconscious mind are what we call needs. The priorities of the conscious mind are what we call wants. We will never get what we want until we've gotten what we need. When you see conflicts and things not happening the way you desire, it's because you're meeting your needs rather than your wants. Most people never ask what the difference is and what their actual needs are that are getting met in these situations.

Research going back fifty years reveals that we don't become consciously aware that something has happened until half a second after it has occurred. The first half a second is all unconscious mind processing and action. What this means is that consciousness is the part farthest away from reality that has the least access to it. Your unconscious mind is the part of you closest to reality, with the truest view of the world—not the conscious mind. The conscious mind gets only whatever the unconscious mind gives it.

So then, how do we give it what it wants?

How do we solve the problem where it is?

CHAPTER 2

SOLVING THE PROBLEM WHERE IT IS

The different levels of your mind are designed to do different things, and you want to solve problems in the part of the mind where they occur. There are two levels of the mind I want you to focus on right now: the *conscious mind* and the *emotional mind*.

The *conscious mind* thinks about what you should and should not do, and about what you want and don't want.

The emotional mind thinks about what's good and bad or right and wrong. It's concerned with deeper meaning.

This is important because we want to make sure we're solving the correct problem on the correct level of your mind.

For example, Stoicism is a framework for navigating life as a conscious construct in the conscious mind. This means that based on these interpretations of reality, this is what these things mean and therefore this is how you should navigate them. We need to understand how to respond to the world, and how to make conscious decisions on what we should and shouldn't do, based on what we want and don't want.

The emotional mind, however, is where the heaviest work is done. This is where we assign meaning to what we experience. Somebody calling you a bad name could mean that they're disrespecting you or that you're not as good as you think you are. By going to the level of your emotional mind, you can correct what things mean. You can draw different conclusions based on the same data so that somebody calling you a bad name means they're having a bad day. Changing that meaning changes how your emotional mind responds to it and how everything else falls into place.

Look at the statement, "If A, then B." If A means *this*, then B means *this*, and we should do *that* in response. The rational mind is operating on the meaning created by the emotional mind. But the meaning itself is *separate* from the emotional mind that creates it.

To correct the programming of a particular level of our mind, we must figure out in which level the problem exists. Is it a conscious mind framework issue? Is it an emotional mind meaning issue? If I have a broken leg, talking about my feelings doesn't solve that problem—I've got to fix my leg. If I'm having trouble losing weight, that could be a conscious mind problem, an emotional mind problem, a physiological problem, or an instinctive mind problem. That's when we do investigative work to figure out where the problem lies.

Much self-help advice—especially for men—tells us that to be valuable, we need to acquire valuable stuff. Well, that's one way to deal with issues in your personal life if you feel insecure. The other way is to fix that insecurity. Instead of spending your earnings on expensive toys just to get the girl, you can fix your insecurity and get what you want in your relationship. Faster, cleaner, cheaper!

How the Minds Think and Solve Problems

Let's now understand how the mind solves problems and makes decisions; it's not what you think. As I shared in the introduction, the mind tries to protect us from ourselves if it cannot trust us to listen to the call to action of our emotions. That's a real mouthful (or brainful), but it becomes easier to grasp.

We don't want our mind to protect us from ourselves, because then we can't allow our consciousness to run the show. If the mind has to constrain us and shape our decision-making, knowing that we're running from perceived pain, it takes away our free will. If your unconscious mind is creating the menu of options that your consciousness is allowed to choose from, and you can't ensure that menu includes the things you want in life, then your unconscious mind is running the show.

Let me introduce you to the OODA loop—observe, orient, decide, act—which is the way the mind processes reality in order to respond to it in the least suboptimal way as it comes. The mind *observes* what's going on, *orients* your place in the situation, *decides* where to go, and then *acts*.

Simple—but not really. Most books, articles, and other efforts to explain the OODA loop fail to account for the unconscious OODA looping that is actually occurring. This unconscious process is, in reality, a nine-step process that occurs in three phases. Let's check it out:

The first phase is the unconscious mind phase.

- In the first step, your unconscious mind receives information from the outside world.
- In step two, your unconscious mind interprets that input and takes any needed immediate action in response.
- In step three, the unconscious mind curates a picture of the world to pass to the conscious mind. This is not only the things you see, hear, touch, taste, and smell but also the emotions you experience and the thoughts you have.

The second phase is the conscious mind phase.

- In step four, your conscious mind receives that collated picture—your perceptions of the world around you, your thoughts, your feelings, your memories—from your unconscious mind.

Remember, you don't consciously become aware of something until half a second after it's occurred.
- In step five, your conscious mind decides what it needs to do in response and passes that back to the unconscious mind for action in step six.

The third phase is the unconscious action phase.

- In step seven, the unconscious mind receives the orders from the conscious mind.
- In step eight, the unconscious mind looks at those orders and compares them to everything it wants and needs, deciding if it's going to comply with the orders or not.
- In step nine, you either take action or not.

Understand what this means given what we now know: If your mind believes it has to protect you from yourself, it's going to take actions without your consent that shape your decisions. The collated picture it gives you will be biased and curated so that your conscious mind won't have the ability to take you in directions your unconscious mind deems harmful.

The OODA loop shows how the unconscious mind processes the world in the observation phase, then creates a menu of choices for you in the orientation phase. The conscious mind makes a decision, then bounces it back to your unconscious mind for action. The important piece to remember is that your conscious mind doesn't get to decide the menu of choices. Your unconscious mind structures the menu by rejecting options it doesn't want you to choose.

The book *The Control Heuristic* by Luca DellAnna goes into that phenomenon much more deeply.[2] There's a structure in your mind called the basal ganglia. This is the gatekeeper to action, where your unconscious mind decides whether to take an action you've given it.

---

2 - Luca DellAnna, *The Control Heuristic: The Nature of Human Behavior*, 2nd ed. (self-pub., 2024).

It does this by weighing the positive and negative emotional associations of previous events with the action you're trying to take. The beliefs you have about yourself and how the world works are what drive the emotional response.

The basal ganglia looks at the different beliefs you have about yourself and the world around you and makes decisions based on those beliefs. The emotion is just the signal. We can see the beliefs, the belief sets, and how those are structured as the algorithm that produces the signal. As a hypnotist, I am way more interested in how the signal is generated than in what the signal is. If I can change how your mind is processing the world, if I can change that observation-orientation phase, I completely change your decision tree, your choice architecture. From a conscious level, I open up all kinds of different opportunities that weren't there before or close off opportunities or roads we don't want to go down, just by changing the choice architecture.

This is an important piece for free will, because if you are not given the opportunity to make a particular choice, then you don't have the free will to do so. This is why people get stuck in the cage or on the treadmill—because their mind does not give them the option or makes it extremely difficult to pursue a particular option. If you are stuck in a cage, you are stuck in relative mediocrity. You're stuck in that place where you can't go after the things you want. You can do stuff that's easy but not challenging. But anything that would take you closer to the realization of the negative thoughts about yourself, about your insecurities, low self-worth, low self-esteem, powerlessness, weakness—anything that would take you toward that, any possible failure would mean you'd go down that dark road. It would be a threat to you, an existential threat.

For the treadmill people, you're never able to get off the treadmill. Your mind has stuck you with a carrot-and-stick situation where you have to run from the pain that's the stick, but you're also being seduced by your unconscious mind with all these nice little dopamine hits and everything else you get from the social affirmation and external validation along the way. So you're running from the stick and toward the carrot. You've got this double motivation there—your mind can use pleasure and rewards to shape your decision-making and behavior. Nobody thinks feeling good is a bad thing, and it definitely can be. Feeling good about something can be a trap.

Consider pretty much every single addiction you can think of. Each one is driven by wanting to feel good because it makes you feel good in the moment. It makes you feel phenomenal—even if that feeling is just numbness, to where you don't feel the pain anymore. Sometimes that's enough to make somebody addicted—just not feeling the pain anymore.

The observation phase is where your mind is processing the world. We can change how it does that using hypnosis. The orientation phase is where the menu of choices is generated from your unconscious mind. We can change how that is created. We can change the decisions you get to make; we are able to change your menu of choices. We get to make it much, much bigger or much, much smaller but only the best ones for you. Then, in the action phase, because we're changing all the belief sets that drive the observation and orientation phases, we can also change how willing your mind is to take action on the decisions you make.

By analyzing, deconstructing, and reassembling these different belief structures on that deep subconscious level, you change all of the hardest parts of the OODA loop. You change all the most difficult things we struggle with when we're trying to get through life the way we want to.

Understanding all this, the temptation is now greatest to reach for rational solutions. *Oh, I rationally understand how my mind works, so I can now rationally reset those aspects of my thinking that I rationally realize are not rationally helpful.* I'm sorry, no; it does not work that way. We can try to make it work—maybe you already have. And yet here you are.

Here's why rational coping strategies don't cure.

CHAPTER 3

STOP COPING AND START CURING

At the beginning of 2021, I declared war on my bullshit. I was done. I decided I was going to figure out what was wrong with me, once and for all. I tried everything. I saw a therapist, did some entrepreneurial coaching, and began working with a mental health group focused on identifying and uprooting limiting beliefs. One day during a session, I had a revelation: My life matters. I was forty-five years old, and I'd never had that thought before.

A few months later, I did some psychedelics. As I sat in my recliner, I realized this was the first time in my life I had ever looked forward. I'd been going through the motions, never anticipating anything. Now I was looking *forward* to the future.

Over the years, I had tried every modality I could to feel better, but nothing touched my core beliefs (like, *I'm not going to get what I want in life.*) I was just addressing surface-level beliefs, like why I was procrastinating—products of the rational mind, not the emotional mind.

These coping mechanisms are addressing the (perceived) negative emotional experience, not the cause of it.

Let's say a woman seeks therapy to overcome her persistent fear. But what if she's afraid because she's regularly subjected to domestic abuse at home? Then her fear is a good thing, and she's not the problem. Yet the therapy (or any other modality) is limited to treating her as the source of both the problem and the solution, even if that's not the case. Is the garden the source of the weed? My point is that coping mechanisms don't go deep enough to uproot beliefs; they're like cutting the stem of a weed and expecting the weed to stop growing.

Modalities That Don't Work (And Why)

A coping mechanism is something that allows you to manage a negative condition of some kind. Here we'll explore the downside of the most common ones.

Cognitive Behavioral Therapy

Cognitive behavioral therapy (CBT) is a beautiful example of something designed as a coping mechanism. CBT is a collection of conscious, deliberate things that you can do to manage your stress, anxiety, fear, depression, or other persistent negative emotions. The problem is that CBT doesn't do anything about what's generating those emotions. It's just a set of tools that allows you to manage the reaction after the emotion is generated. After unconscious mind observation, unconscious mind orientation, and then signal generation, CBT becomes step four. But once you're in your conscious mind, that's where all the work is happening—and your consciousness responds to these different emotions and stressors.

As a result, the only thing you're doing is finding ways to numb, medicate, run away from, and otherwise disassociate from these negative emotions. Disassociating is a coping mechanism.

Psychotherapy

Psychotherapy is a little different. It's about understanding why things happen and what you could have done differently. But there are several problems with this. First, the rational mind is concerned with details. That's how it manages to do the amazing things it does—it focuses on details and differentiates between different traumatic events in the past. Each individual event is an individual trauma, an individual problem to be solved. Psychotherapy deals with problems on a rational level, trying to understand it from a logical perspective and attempting to come up with better ways of dealing with the situation should it occur again.

The issue is that decisions are made in the instinctive mind and in the emotional mind. Psychotherapy doesn't change the meaning of any of those events.

The lowest you can get in the stack of minds, so to speak, is the rational mind. You can deal with things in the rational mind, gain a new rational understanding, and manage your emotional responses a bit better with some decision-making strategies. Which is great. Don't get me wrong. Having some understanding of what things work can lessen the emotional blow. But this doesn't help you change your unconscious beliefs.

When we talk about the OODA loop—observe, orient, decide, act—we're not doing anything for the observation-orientation phase. We're focusing only on the decision phase.

Psychedelic-Assisted Psychotherapy

Psychedelic-assisted psychotherapy is a slightly different beast. It combines the limitations of both psychedelics and psychotherapy. The beautiful thing about psychedelic-assisted psychotherapy is that it allows you to get that direct access to your unconscious mind and to see things from a deeper perspective.

The problem is that a psychotherapist is still doing standard psychotherapy while you're on the medicine. You don't have a choice in what you get to see, and whatever comes up is what you deal with in that moment. You're still reframing it from a rational perspective rather than from an emotional one.

Sure, you'll get a deeper level of insight into slightly bigger themes. You can make changes on that emotional-instinctive level. But it's still just exploring the scene through the lens of rationality. You're not able to figure out what the beliefs are that drive your obstacles. I've never done psychedelic-assisted psychotherapy, but I have done psychedelic-assisted coaching. You have someone there to help you navigate the things that come up, meaning you can do some change work with the door open, which is not possible when you're doing psychedelics on your own.

Overall, psychedelic-assisted psychotherapy gets a thumbs-up from me, but most practitioners can't get down to those unconscious beliefs, and because you can't control what you see, it's less targeted than hypnotic work.

Psychedelics

As for psychedelics themselves, they're an amazing discovery tool. They drag up from your unconscious mind whatever you need to deal with the most at that point in time. They make you look at things differently. They show you things that make you ask questions you'd never thought of.

There's potential in psychedelics as a therapy, but the problem is that you don't get to do any processing or integration while you're on them (unless you're working with a coach or a therapist while you're on your trip). You're stuck doing interpretation with the beliefs you already have, which can reinforce your current coping mechanisms because you interpret things in a way that's favorable to ego.

They can get you stuck in building a more beautiful treadmill or a more spacious cage. That's the problem with psychedelics—you're still stuck in the cage, you're still stuck on the treadmill, and they won't get you out of either of those traps.

Somatic Techniques

Somatic techniques are great for helping process your emotions. I love these as provocation tools. Somatic body work and breath work force things to the surface through the idea that emotions are energy. They need to move, to complete their process—this energy is your body preparing to take action of some kind. If that process is interrupted, then your emotions aren't fully processed. Somatic breath work shows you what's not processed so that you can allow the energy to move the way it needs to in order to complete its action. It's freakin' beautiful.

I don't do breath work anymore because the last session I did affected my neurochemistry and increased the side effects of the medication I'm on. Breath work fundamentally causes neurochemical changes, and that's what it's designed to do.

We're getting into a little woo-woo space, but if you're reading a book like *The Body Keeps the Score*,[3] there's a lot to be said for using somatic work to help you figure out what you haven't yet processed on an emotional level. I still don't think it does anything to change the beliefs that you have. If you've got a backpack with fifty pounds of crap in it, somatic work can take out ten to fifteen pounds of it. It's going to be a lot easier for you to move around with less weight, but it won't change anything fundamental about you, your belief set, or how you navigate through the world.

---

3 - Bessel van der Kolk, *The Body Keeps the Score: Brain, Mind, and Body in the Healing of Trauma* (New York: Penguin Books, 2014).

State Change

State change refers to any activity that forces your physical and mental state to change by the very act of doing the thing. Think exercise and cold plunges, for example. Both may be useful for the physical health benefits, but state change allows you to crank up positive, happy neurochemicals in your brain. This manufactures a positive emotional state, which does two things.

First, it convinces you that you're doing the right thing, that this is the way to go, because you're moving toward pleasure and away from pain. It starts locking you into particular solution sets.

Second, it drowns out the negative signals that you need to be hearing. If you have problems in your life, you must be able to see the check engine light come on. If you're doing all this physical activity to feel good, chasing that dopamine hit all the time, you're putting a piece of masking tape over the check engine light.

State change is not necessarily dangerous, but you've got to ensure that you're doing it for the right reason. If you're going to the gym because you're a bodybuilder and you're in competition, that makes total sense. If you're doing it to get fit or to maintain your muscle mass in your old age, that also makes total sense. If you're there to dodge your emotional issues, you'll do more harm than good. The bodybuilding world is rife with people who are broken and depressed, and the gym is their only way to hang on.

As for those cold plunges, you've got that whole ego thing. You get the massive dopamine hit and you get to play, "Oh, look at me, I'm doing all these hard, difficult things. I've got discipline!" If you couldn't tell anybody that you did it, would you still do it? Without those ego hits of dopamine, probably not.

The physiological forcing of moods is not a good idea, in my opinion. That doesn't mean don't exercise or don't do cold plunges. But if you're doing that as a way to manage your emotional state, you're doing the right thing for the wrong reason.

Meditation

Meditation is another intervention that is causing more harm than good in myriad ways. For example, I've got a beef with Eckhart Tolle and ilk like him who teach that you are not your thoughts or your emotions. Bullshit. Complete and total bullshit.

When you try to create stillness in your mind through disassociation, you're teaching yourself to disassociate from your emotions and thoughts—and only the negative ones. Tolle and teachers like him say, basically, "Oh, the negative thoughts are part of the mind, but all these positive things—joy and everything else—are from a deeper part, from 'Source,' and that's from God. And so we should definitely be in that place all the time."

Think about this: What you're doing with such meditation is disassociating yourself from important, helpful signals. You can't get the signal that something's wrong from your mind because you're disassociating from it, you're running from it, you're ignoring it, and you're suppressing it, which means two things:

1. You don't know what the problems are.
2. You're telling your mind that you can't help it solve these problems, which means, all of a sudden, bigger and bigger areas of your mind and emotions (and life) become off-limits from your own help. How fucked up is that?

Notice how people who meditate a lot live simple lives; that's the level of complexity they can navigate when they're telling their mind they can't help it in any other way. The flip side is that they're trying to feel blissful all the time, which gets them in that pleasure trap. They're basically saying to themselves, *I can't handle things that are hard in the world. I just want to be as high as a kite all the time.* And so you're getting high on your own supply, as a meditator. Training your mind to do that is dangerous. It's massively limiting. It changes what choices you can make because you can't do anything negative, and you can't feel anything negative. Your mind can't lead you to anything that would be hard—hard and yet helpful.

That said, I did about six months of training on Buddhist meditation called TWIM, which stands for tranquil wisdom insight meditation. You're supposed to be focused on cultivating loving kindness in your heart, compassion for others, and the like—it's about learning how to let go of your thoughts of judgment as they pass by. You notice each one, recognize it, smile again, and return to your focus on the "metta" of life. It teaches how to push distractions out of your mind, which is good.

But with the TWIM practice, they were careful to do two things with me and all others who learn this lesser-known meditation form:

1. One of the things they say is that you can't ignore an emotion. Feelings are not something you can just make go away, which is good because it means you can still feel all the things, which means you can still get all the signals.
2. They also say that if a thought keeps coming back, then it's something important you need to pay attention to. So it's not getting rid of all thoughts; it's getting rid of the flitting distractions that come through there.

I do think meditation is beautiful for doing things like that. I also think it's beautiful for exploring the limits of consciousness. As you start working through that TWIM meditation, as you start building up your skill in it, you get into some of the deeper *jhanas* of meditation. One day, two days in a row, I did a TWIM meditation where I dropped down to the seventh *jhana*, which is that space of nonperception where consciousness is just floating in nothingness. When you're no longer aware of your body, you're no longer aware of your breathing, you're no longer aware of anything around you. Consciousness is just . . .

floating. In nothing. And when I came back from those meditations, I felt like I was on mushrooms for two or three hours afterward. My mind was fundamentally altered as if I had been on a psychedelic trip, just through meditation. The fact that consciousness can separate itself so far from the inputs of reality, that this is just focusing on floating around in nothing, is fascinating—and cool. Meditation as a tool to explore the nature of consciousness is great, just like using psychedelics to explore the nature of reality is.

But if you're using meditation to learn how to disassociate from your emotions and your thoughts, if you're learning how to make yourself high all the time, there's some danger there. There are some things you need to be careful of and cautious about when you're using meditation in that way.

Medications

The last thing I want to touch on is medications. I mean that both ways. It's difficult because I'm not a doctor, I'm not a mental health professional, and I'm not a psychiatrist. But I'll say two things because I can't help myself.

The first is that if you have a psychological or neurological condition, you need support of some kind to function normally. I have low dopamine, and I have high serotonin. I've got a couple of other neurochemical imbalances that mean my baseline state is not where it needs to be. Some stuff is too low; some stuff is way too high. I got tested to figure out what was going on with my body before I started pushing buttons via drugs. I figured out where I was deficient and where I had an overabundance of things, and I targeted medication and other support to bring things more into balance based on actual data. So from that perspective, if you have an actual condition—if you have ADHD, if you have bipolar disorder, if you have severe depression, whatever it happens to be—number one, get data. Figure out what is happening on a neurochemical neurotransmitter level, on genetic methylation pathways. There are all kinds of tests you can do to determine what's going on in your body and why your body is processing things the way it is. If you have an issue, do the testing to get the actual data and then target the interventions to the things you need to correct.

When you do things that way, medication is a phenomenal tool. But it can take a while to dial it in and nail it. Do it as a data-based, evidence-based, targeted approach. Don't just start taking things because you think, *Everyone's taking methylene blue on the internet these days. I've got to try it because they say it's amazing.* Or, *Oh, everybody's talking about mitochondrial health. I've got to do like thirty-seven different supplements to support my mitochondria—or was it midichlorians?*

Maybe you don't. And maybe taking those supplements is going to mess you up. It definitely has for me in the past. If you are in a severe situation, any support you can get to help you out of that moment is useful. When you're using medication as a targeted intervention, when there is a serious problem, it is beautiful. But when the psychiatrist I was working with found out I had bipolar, he put me on lithium, which cranked my dopamine to nothing and made me feel suicidal. That was not good. Two and a half weeks into it, I called with that update. But he suggested I keep going because it was just a normal part of the process. No, more like dangerous as hell.

But again, I personally know there is value in medication as an intervention. Another psychiatrist hit me with an antipsychotic to knock me out of a manic state during a rough episode. Medication makes sure I can sleep the way I need to. Sometimes your neurochemistry is just not normal, and you have to do things to bring it back into balance. But it always has to be done from a data-based, evidence-based perspective. Anything else, and you're just playing a potentially deadly guessing game. It's way too easy to mess somebody up that way.

Anything else and you're rolling the dice, especially with neurochemical stuff, because so much can go wrong. So much. Don't mess with your brain unless you know what the hell you're doing. Make sure you've got the data to support what you're doing, including the most important data of all—how it changes you as soon as you're on it.

On Pain Relief

When you're in pain, doing something to make the pain go away is probably good. When you break your leg, there's no point in not taking Advil or aspirin to make yourself feel better. I had appendicitis, and they wanted to give me fentanyl or morphine. I was in massive agony. And they knew it. But the difference was, rather than just mask the pain, it was figuring out what the pain was trying to tell me, then cranking down the pain. Because we already know what we need to do. And that's why we need to be so careful about using coping mechanisms—you have to follow the pain to the problem first. Because if you kill the pain before you figure out what the problem is, you can't deal with the problem. If you shut down the emotion before you determine what it's trying to help you with, what problem it's trying to solve, you can't solve the problem. You don't know what's going on. You've got to sit in the signal long enough to figure out what you need to do. Then you can do something to lessen the pain and make it go away.

The beautiful thing about dealing with emotions, the way that I teach people to do it, is the default state—the default response to any negative emotion—is to get curious. It's asking you for help to solve a particular type of problem. So get curious. Because as soon as you're curious, you're not feeling so bad anymore because you're doing the right thing. Let the emotion move through you. If you're sad, go ahead and cry. Have that thing. And when it's done, get curious. Because that puts you in a fundamentally different state. You're doing a completely different thing and you're doing the right thing. Because you're helping your mind solve the problem. There's no reason or need for your mind to keep yelling at you with that emotion, to keep blasting you with that emotion anymore. It's got your attention. You're doing the right thing; you're helping it the way you need to. The negative emotion goes away, but it does so because you're solving the problem. Not because you're getting high on your own supply, not because you're physiologically forcing it, not because you taught yourself to disassociate—it's because you're doing the right thing and not the wrong thing.

All that said, many of the tools covered in this chapter can be used to process emotion and move that which is stuck. But they don't touch the core beliefs—so you will be constantly subjected to the negative emotions you've been trying to avoid all along. Let's touch on those core beliefs.

Let's do a lot more than that.

CHAPTER 4

HOW BELIEFS CONTROL EVERYTHING

Esteemed evolutionary biologist Bret Weinstein took part in a debate at Oxford University on the subject of religion, as one does.[4] Bret stated that most animals have only one way to pass information from one generation to the next—genetics. Humans, on the other hand, have a second way: We tell stories. And religion is a collection of stories to be passed to future generations and is meant to convey *metaphorical truth* (although that is not explicitly stated in the conveyance of those stories). Metaphorical truth refers to claims that are not literally true, but if we *behave* as if they are true, we will get better results in our lives.

Bret gives the example of a tsunami that slammed Malaysia, causing all manner of death and destruction. Thousands were killed and scores more were injured in this disaster. But there was one group of villages on the coast where nobody got hurt. Even though they were nearest the danger zone, and even though their villages were indeed completely wiped out, not one villager was injured or killed. Why?

It turns out that this local tribe had a myth about an angry sea goddess. The story goes that on occasion, this sea goddess entered a fit

---

4 - Alister McGrath and Bret Weinstein, "Religion: Useful Fiction or Ultimate Truth? Part 1," September 13, 2019, in *The Big Conversation*, podcast, MP3 audio, 01:10:12, www.youtube.com/watch?v=kRx2uNMJFnU.

of rage and destroyed the villages. Whenever she started to get angry, there were visible signs: The water would start to boil and recede. It turns out that a bubbling sensation in the water *is* a physical sign that a tsunami is coming, and to this tribe, this sign of impending doom, among others, was encoded in mythology. When the people saw these signs, they knew it was time to run for the hills (literally).

Was it true that the angry sea goddess was coming to wipe out the village and kill everyone? No. But codifying the signs of a tsunami in myth proved extremely useful for those villagers.

Another similar useful belief is that of an omnipresent, all-seeing God. When people feel like they're being watched, they tend to follow the rules more. In psychology, this is called the observer effect. If you believe that there's an all-present God who sees you even when nobody else can and who is going to judge you after you're dead on what you did and did not do, you'll witness the observer effect in your everyday life.

Religion instills the observer effect into every single person who follows it because they'll always feel that they're being watched and judged by God even if they can get away with certain actions in the physical realm where no other person may be watching them. From a social perspective, that's an incredibly useful belief. It's as if beliefs are tools—which they are.

Let's reframe beliefs as things, so if we act as if certain helpful beliefs are true (even if they are literally not), we may get better results. Good tools!

Another point about these belief tools. A belief is something that doesn't need to be proven, and it is often believed despite evidence to the contrary. If you already believe something, you don't feel the need to prove it. I don't feel the need to prove I'm a man or a hypnotist—I already believe those things to be true. So if you feel a need to prove something to yourself, *you don't believe it yet*. Which means your unconscious will ignore all proof, because it doesn't believe what

CHAPTER 4 - HOW BELIEFS CONTROL EVERYTHING

you're trying to prove. If you believe the earth is flat, you're believing that in spite of evidence to the contrary, and no one can persuade you that it's round (well, no one but a hypnotist).

If beliefs are assertions that are felt as true without evidence and even in spite of evidence to the contrary, that means *beliefs are a part of the unconscious mind*. Understand that? They *must* be behind that critical factor that's rejecting the evidence to the contrary, doing so based on whether or not it matches what we *already* believe. So it doesn't matter whether these beliefs conform to physical reality. The key takeaway is that helpful tool beliefs increase our chance of survival and give us better results, either on an individual or on a social level. The truth of them matters not. All we want is helpfulness.

How do we create these helpful beliefs?

Everyone is already creating beliefs on their own, individually, all the time. My job as a hypnotist is to navigate and observe that belief formation environment. When I watch other people, I draw my own conclusions about what these beliefs are and what they mean; that is, how helpful or unhelpful they are.

As I said earlier, most humans learn through observation thanks to the mirror neurons. There's a *huge* survival advantage of being able to understand how to navigate the world by watching people who are doing it successfully. A four-year-old child doesn't know much about how the world works. But they're surrounded by adults, and whatever they're doing is working well enough to keep them alive—and that is useful information to a child. But this mirroring-learning business is an automatic, unconscious mechanism by which we derive meaning from the world; this is how our beliefs are formed. We do this all the time, 24/7/365, without even realizing it. As we observe the world and other people in it, we extract meaning from everything we encounter.

In the earliest stage of our lives, we have only one way of getting help: cry. A human infant has that one signal to draw attention from their caregiver and get something they need. Whether they're hungry, wet, cold, lonely, or just unhappy, there's only one proper response. The infant's parents respond to that cry of distress in the same way: they come over, investigate, and attempt to fix the problem.

From a young age, all such distress is treated the same. But as we get a little bit older, we start hearing things like "You hurt my feelings" and "She broke my heart." Maybe someone says, "You made me so angry. Why did you do this to me?" Notice what, exactly, happens—instinctive negative emotional expression (crying) that was intended to be a signal for help (from the parents or caregiver) fades away. Mirror neurons happen. We hear adults and older children liken emotions to pain and pain to identity crisis. And so we come to believe that emotions are the same as pain and pleasure. Physical pleasure feels good and happiness feels good, therefore it's easy to equate happiness and physical pleasure. It's a story that makes sense to a developing mind.

Now think about all the stories that people around us are telling, right now. How do we derive meaning from them? How do we act in response? Some people try to help you derive metaphorical truths, but it's important to recognize that we're deriving those on our own. We may test them in the environment, revising our beliefs as a result of what we experience into something that more closely comports with observed reality.

That said, the belief that something is wrong with you or that you're the problem is a tricky one when it comes to testing and measuring. Until a certain point of development, we humans are incredibly self-centered. Our brains literally cannot see other people as separate beings before nine months of age, which means up until a certain point of our development, everything *has* to be our fault because it can't possibly be anybody else's because there is nobody else! This means we start thinking early on, quite naturally, that what's going on is our fault. What if nobody corrects that over time?

Consider phrases like "What's wrong with you?," which implies that you're a bad person. Who you are is bad; it is wrong in some way, shape, or form. That is reinforced by other stories (experiences and the meaning we draw from them) as we grow up. Ever heard a parent, caregiver, or teacher say, "You brought this on yourself" or "Why are you making me do this to you?" That is reinforcement of the initial organically formed belief.

And then, over time, beliefs form overarching narratives about who we are as people and how we should act in a given situation. Low-resolution beliefs run at the deepest levels of mind and are processed quite quickly. Those are then translated into higher-resolution beliefs (from "I'm not deserving" to "I'm fat/broke/stupid," for example). That then results in *acting* in ways that confirm that consistently. The belief is a tool and not a helpful one!

Or is it?

Consider this: The part of your brain that created that original low-level belief is there to keep you alive, not keep you happy (that's not even its goal!). In fact, if you being unhappy means you are likely to survive, then guess what? The shitty belief is a tool to keep you alive.

Oh no!

The utility of any belief matters a lot more than its literal truth. If a belief is useful for navigating our environment, helping us survive, and getting what we want, then whether or not it is factually true matters less. This is not a judgment; this is a description of the situation. It's not like we're able to investigate all these beliefs anyway with tools from our day-to-day environment. We often don't know what the guiding beliefs are that we're running because it's not happening with conscious input; it's happening on an unconscious level.

Consider basic communication theory, which is as follows: You've got a sender, you've got a receiver, and you've got a message. I, as a sender, want to convey something to you. So I craft a certain message and send it your way, then you interpret it. But I as a sender have no way to control how you interpret it. I don't have the ability to make sure that you draw the right conclusions or the conclusions that

I want you to. I can craft the message as best I can to lead you to that conclusion, but I don't have control over it because the interpretation is entirely up to you.

This point about control is key. Understand that control is about safety, and safety is about fear. *If I control everything, I can keep my worst fears from happening and make my best wishes come true.* It's fear either way—the fear of unfortunate events or the fear of missing out. If you control enough factors, you control the outcome. But the issue is that you don't have control over anything but yourself: your actions. You do not control the outcome. Try to, and you try to make everything a rational process, not an emotional one (which it is). Control strategies don't work because you don't have control. You only have influence. And influence is enough. Including influence over what happens inside your brain. You have more control over that than you might think.

This is important when it comes to reviewing our beliefs because they're not done *to us*. I will say it again. *Beliefs are not things that happen to us.* They're things that we derive on our own.

Mirror neurons play their role as we grow up, yes—when it comes to behaviors. But the beliefs we develop and the stories we tell ourselves are all our doing. That said, we *are* deriving them based on observing our environment; we're deriving them based on what other people are doing and saying. We're using them as part of the hypothesis formation and testing process in order to be a human in our world. But again, nobody tells us *what* to believe. We have to reach that on our own. The unconscious mind has free will, so it doesn't have to accept what's being said. But if it doesn't have any better conclusion or any better data, all it can say is, in effect, *This doesn't feel right, but this is what I'm being told, and I don't know any better. I guess we should go with this for now. I will probably stay alive if I act as if this is true.*

CHAPTER 4 - HOW BELIEFS CONTROL EVERYTHING

If there is a belief set that helps me navigate life better, I grab it. The difficulty, of course, is that until you disprove the old belief, you now have *two* sets of beliefs in your mind, and your mind has to decide which one of those belief sets to use. The old belief set has a lot more evidence, as it has been around a lot longer. It has more justification as a stronger foundation than the new one has. So the old one usually wins *unless* the new one is constantly reinforced, which is why repetitive hypnotic work helps. But you don't have to do that if you dismantle the older, unhelpful belief set. If you are able to disprove and remove the old belief set by disqualifying it, then there's immediate space for the new set to drop in without any opposition.

I do *not* mean to say we should try to change what happened to cause that initial belief set. Here's why this bears repeating:

The mind is trying to help you solve problems, but in doing so, it can create more problems. The goal is to understand what initial problem the mind is trying to solve by holding you back. To do this, we must come to understand the emotional belief set, then reframe it *without* changing anything about what happened. New beliefs *must* conform to the existing understanding of what happened in the past—just explain what happened in a different way.

When you're young, you have no control over the environment or the game being played. You are not able to get what you need; you are not able to get it right because the game can't be won—the rules keep changing. Thus, you can't derive any information about yourself from those results. If the game is rigged, losing is the expected outcome. Thus, losing doesn't mean you're broken or that there's something wrong with you. You simply played a game designed to create a loss. That's not your fault. "Don't blame the player, blame the game," the saying goes.

Caregivers who are wounded or who went through a lot growing up and didn't do the work to fix it end up unable to deal with the world in a healthy way. They take out their issues on everyone around them, particularly children (like you and me, as kids). Their behavior was about their own issues—it didn't have anything to do with you or with what you did or didn't do. So you can't draw any conclusions about yourself from their maladaptive behaviors. There is nothing wrong with you.

It could also be that other children were the causes of ultimately unhelpful beliefs that were based on just downright awful experiences. I had one client who shared with me that everything at home was fine, but at school, he was constantly bullied, ostracized, and abused. All the negative emotion he felt was due to his peers.

Then there was another client who grew up in a relatively poor neighborhood, but his parents provided for him as best they could. He simply grew up in the ghetto. For that particular client, the belief system fix was to show him that his parents didn't have the capacity to give him what he needed in that early childhood and adolescent environment. If I ask a friend for $1,000 and they have only $17 in their checking account, they don't have the capability to give me $1,000. They'd probably give me everything they have, but I'd still be $983 short. The client began to understand that not getting what he needed wasn't a reflection of his worth—it just wasn't available to him in his environment.

Is it exactly rational to equate growing up in the ghetto to asking a friend for money? No, not exactly. It's a metaphor, but it's not entirely logical. And that's all right. Good, in fact. Rational belief change doesn't entirely work. I will explain, as this, too, is critical.

How Not to Change Beliefs

Your left brain, the rational brain, is concerned about the trees. Your right brain, the emotional mind, is concerned about the forest. By taking a rational approach to trying to solve the problems with our emotional state, we're trying to chop down trees. We're playing

CHAPTER 4 - HOW BELIEFS CONTROL EVERYTHING

trauma whack-a-mole, to put it another way. You're trying to chop down trees in this forest to make the forest go away. But how many trees do you have to chop down before the forest starts to look *different*? A hell of a lot. How many trees do you have to cut down to make the forest *go away*? All of them. You have to chop down *all* the trees, which is why this feels like a never-ending process because it is a never-ending process.

If you're taking the rationalist approach, understand that every single day of your life, more stuff happens, so more trees get planted that have to be dealt with (cut down). The forest is constantly replenishing itself with more and more trees, providing more and more examples of why this overall emotional conclusion, the forest, is existent and true.

The rationalist approach never, ever, ever ends; this is why you have to change things on the this-is-what-the-forest-looks-like level. You must address the *entire* forest itself rather than the individual trees because you're never going to run out of individual trees to cut down; the little bastards just grow way too fast for this one-at-a-time sawing and wood chipping. The forest is always going to be there if you take the rationalist left-brain approach.

All right then. Let's raze the forest.

Then replant it.

CHAPTER 5

REWRITE THE PAST

I have a problem with something.
You know this idea that we could and should change the past? There are several techniques, methods, and so on that purport to be able to change the nature of the past from your memory recall perspective.

Because you're having a hard time and keep getting triggered, why don't we just go back to your past and reimagine how it should have gone? Then we'll use that as your memory—your new memory. Let's go back and reparent you while we're at it. You weren't able to get what you needed from your parents at the time. We'll just go ahead and give that younger version of you the thing it was missing.

Do you foresee the problem with this set of tactics? What you're doing is trying to change the past by giving yourself what you didn't get at that time and then trying to make it work out the way you wanted to. Or trying to imagine the things you would rather have said.

A lot of these reimagine-the-past techniques try to change the *facts* of what happened in the past. To include something that wasn't there, to make a decision you didn't make, to say things you didn't say, to do things you didn't do, and to reimagine things going well as a result. This addresses only the rational mind concept of the past (the facts of what happened) and not the emotional perspective. Also, it's *a lie*—and we *know* it's a lie.

The mind does not and cannot actually change those memories. It remembers what happened. It knows that one thing is true (what went down) and one thing is false (what the therapist tries to trick your imagination into pretending happened). The latter is fantasy. You know. You can't let go of reality. To attempt to do so is to tell yourself, *I want to live a lie. The reality is too painful. I don't like what happened. I don't want that to be the truth. I want to live a fantasy. I want to live a lie.*

Then your mind realizes, *OK, this is something I can't deal with. This memory, this event, and anything like them before or since are all threats to my existence.*

Welcome to a deep, dark hole.

The reality is that even if you reparent yourself now and give yourself what you didn't have back then, you didn't have it back then and nothing you can do is going to change that fact. Forget about what you *wish* it was. What did it *mean*? That is the more interesting question. What *could* it mean instead? Even more interesting. If we're focused on an aspect of a memory and what we wish it was, we're not looking at the meaning. We're not trying to change the meaning, to understand what happened and its ramifications from a different, helpful-tool perspective. But if you tell your mind, *I don't like this memory; give me a different one*, you are showing yourself to be incapable of handling reality. This will make it harder to solve present and future problems consciously or unconsciously because you have proven that you are a weak, childish, unreliable person. *Don't show me reality because I can't handle it.* Deep, dark hole, indeed.

Dealing with a past we perceive as painful has to be, fundamentally and simply, understanding the past in a different way—meaning we will ultimately be changing the beliefs we've formed from those events rather than trying to change the events themselves or pretend we could have done things differently. Which brings up something else: I assume that at every single point in time, I have done the best

I possibly could in any particular situation. I made the best possible decision that was available to me at the time, given what I understood at the time, given what I believed about myself at the time. It doesn't do any good to know now what I should have done then, because I didn't know what to do then, so it doesn't freakin' help me. Another trap; another lie.

Yet many men go on thinking that if they can change the past, they can change their present. *I don't like where I'm at. Where I'm at is the result of all the things I've done. So if I can change the things I've done, then I'll be in a different place right now. I won't feel the way I do right now.*

We can't change what happened, but we can learn different lessons. We can assign different meanings. We can create different beliefs from those same events. And that's where the magic happens.

Reframing without Lying

It doesn't matter if you can take care of yourself and protect yourself now, for example, if you were victimized when you were five. Being able to protect yourself now doesn't mean you could protect yourself back then. And so it is with any haunting memory. We've got to find a way to make that old event a win in some way, shape, or form. We need to make it *mean* that you were strong and capable, not powerless and weak in that moment. That is the only way we can move on from our past: *We have to figure out how we won.* How we navigated that situation successfully. How what we did was exactly the right thing to do, given what we had available at the time. No need to go off trying to reimagine a different past, trying to reparent yourself, trying to give yourself what you didn't have, trying to say the thing you could have said, trying to figure out what you should have done instead. In fact, trying to figure out what you should have done instead is a great way to keep on punishing yourself forever—because you didn't know what you should have done because you didn't do what you should have done!

Look . . . at every point in time, you are the best version of yourself. Because if you could be any better than you would've been, you would've done it better. If you could have done things differently, you would've done things differently. At any point in time, you're making the best possible choices you can, given who you are and what you've been through. So you're always the best version of yourself.

Understanding this—the need to change the past or move on from it and forget it—well, that *need* starts to become a *want*. What you've been carrying around starts to feel a little lighter. Because you don't have a time machine. And that begins to feel . . . OK. Yeah. It's OK.

You don't have to change your past to change your future and your present. Because the things that happened don't matter. It's the meaning that we assign to those events, the lessons we take from those events, that matters. If I got hit by a car, I could define it as good or bad. That's my choice. It's harder to define it as a good thing, I'll admit. I'm not saying, *Oh, I got hit by a car. Best thing that ever happened to me.* There's a famous study on lottery winners and disabled people that discovered that a year later—after the lotto win and the debilitating accident, respectively—both groups reported relative levels of happiness.[5] Not what you would expect!

After the event happened, of course, there was an adjustment. But fundamentally, the point is, the things that happened don't matter nearly as much as we'd expect—even in the case of the world's greatest luck *and* in the worst case of tragedies. It's the lessons we learn from those events that matter.

For example, if you grew up in a poor neighborhood and didn't have what you needed, there's nothing you can do to change the fact that you grew up in a poor neighborhood and couldn't get what

---

[5] - Melissa Dahl, "A Classic Psychological Study on Why Winning the Lottery Won't Make You Happier," The Cut, January 13, 2016, www.thecut.com/2016/01/classic-study-on-happiness-and-the-lottery.html#.

you needed. But you can change what that means about you. You can change the narrative. *Yeah, I grew up that way, so I will make sure it never happens again to me or to my children.* See? The past is accepted for what it was—no lies, no reparenting nonsense—*and* you're able to reframe the meaning. You can change the meaning. Not to change what happened but to change how you feel about it or what it means to you. By shifting the meaning, you change your emotional response now and forever. Because you've changed your *beliefs* as to what those events mean to you.

It's easy. That's what I do every single day with my clients—this reframing work with their memories.

How I Teach Self-Talk

The way I usually set this up for the first session with a new client is to say something like the following (we'll call this sample client Joe). And we go on from here:

> OK, you've been undermining yourself, sabotaging yourself, holding yourself back. You've not been allowing yourself to succeed and go after the things you want in life. Your unconscious mind is doing this for a reason. It's trying to help you in some way, trying to solve a problem of some kind. So you're not really self-sabotaging; you're helping yourself. Because that's fundamentally the purpose of the unconscious mind. It's not there to sabotage you. It's there to help you survive and navigate the world. The unconscious mind is not the enemy.
>
> Today we're going to ask your unconscious mind to help us out a bit more to understand the problems it's trying to solve by holding you back.

Find me a moment in time, a memory, that's going to show me the problem you're trying to solve with this behavior. Not the cause of it. Just the problem you're trying to solve.

OK, so you were a kid. It happened on the playground. Billy pushed you down, he took your Lunchables, and everybody laughed. Got it.

So that's what happened. But how did you feel about what was happening at that moment? Not necessarily the emotions you were experiencing *then*, but how do you feel about the situation *now*? Obviously you feel it's unfair. Of course. Everybody laughing at you. Outcast, right?

How did you feel about yourself at that moment? Powerless, weak, not good enough. Nobody likes you. You're not safe. You can't protect yourself. Yeah. Ouch.

OK, now let's step back from all that. Fill in the blank for me:

I'm the part of Joe who holds Joe back and won't let him succeed. I'm the part of Joe who sabotages him. I'm the part of Joe who won't leave and let him try. And I do this for Joe because . . .

To make sure Joe doesn't get hurt? OK.

To make sure Joe doesn't feel bad? Got it.

To make sure Joe doesn't feel ostracized? Interesting.

And if all that does occur, what happens then?

The dark place. The despair. The depression.

But fundamentally, that part of Joe is just trying to keep Joe alive, right then and there in the presence of Billy the bully. Isn't that right?

Let me tell you something. The unconscious mind is always focused on the present moment. It doesn't have second and third order effects. The solutions that are implemented are designed to solve the problem at the moment without necessarily taking into account how that solution has negative impacts on bigger systems or down the road.

If you feel sad, eat a doughnut to feel better. That's an effective instantaneous solution. But if you're depressed for a year and you're eating a dozen doughnuts a day, all of a sudden you're 350 pounds with a completely different set of problems. Your unconscious mind, of course, is not capable of creating solutions on that timeline. Always focused on the present, remember? It's not capable of creating long-term effective solutions that take into account all the pluses and minuses.

That's a hell of a trap. If Joe goes out there, does what he wants, tries to get what he wants and then he fails, it feels bad, and he ends up in the dark place, which sucks. But it's every day. And yet if he doesn't go out there, he also feels like he's not good enough. He's powerless; he can't have what he wants and doesn't deserve it either. By holding him back, that part of Joe is hurting him more every day without intending to.

You see, when Joe was growing up, no matter what he did, no matter how he tried, he just couldn't get it right. He just never got what he needed. If he's trying stuff and trying stuff and trying stuff and nothing works and nothing works and nothing works, after a while, it's easy to start feeling like . . . maybe it's not the things I'm doing that are wrong; maybe there's just something wrong *with me*.

It's almost like you're playing a game. A game where the rules are always changing; the goalposts are always moving. And if the rules are always changing, and the goalposts are always moving, there's no way to win that game. Is there? You could be the most brilliant, most amazing, most handsome man on the planet, but you still can't win.

So if you cannot win a game that cannot be won, does that tell you anything about who you are or how good you are? Is there something wrong with you that you cannot win a game that cannot be won? Well, no. Because if the game is rigged, then losing is the expected outcome.

When you're young, you don't get to choose the game you play. Your parents can't just pick up and move to a different home. You can't get new parents. You're stuck playing whatever game you're playing. But does that have anything to do with you? No.

So Billy knocked you down, he took your Lunchables, then everybody laughed at you. Kids who are bullies grow up in bad households. If you're growing up in that environment, you get rage. You're always looking for a way to take it out on someone or something. Well, you can't do that against your parents. What happens is you end up taking it out on other people. Does that have anything to do with you? No. That's just Billy taking it out on whoever happens to be convenient.

Now think about guys like Martin Luther King or Gandhi. Their superpower was being able to take everything the world threw at them and saying, "What else you got?" And in doing that, being able to endure everything the world could throw at them, they brought empires to their knees, didn't they? They changed the course of history. Does that sound powerless and weak to you? No, of course not. It takes strength, resilience, and internal fortitude to be able to endure what comes your way.

So I wonder . . . I wonder if you can understand that that's *exactly* what you were doing for yourself, protecting and taking care of yourself as best you could with the tools you had at the time. Just enduring what had to come your way because you didn't have any other options. Does that sound powerless and weak? No. Not at all. So what we now know is that it's not you; you're not powerless and weak. You can protect yourself. You can take care of yourself.

And that's how I usually work with clients to reframe situations and reach different conclusions. It's a lot of fun. For me and for them.

Most clients I work with have completely different life stories, and yet the same pernicious beliefs antagonize almost all of them. Let's discover what can be done to reframe the past events that created those belief sets to see if we can find a newer, more empowering meaning that leaves the past behind without changing it.

Specific Beliefs We All Want Changed

This is not an exhaustive list, but for the person stuck believing them, life is exhausting. Let's make your burden light now.

Different

If you felt different and were excluded because of it, I suggest using a reframe along these lines:

> How many movies do you know that are about normal people? How many books have you read about normal people? Everyone wants to be unique, special, different. Nobody wants to be normal. And that's what you are, isn't it? Unique? Special? Different? That would mean you're the person everyone else wants to be.

Try it.

Excluded

If you felt like you were always excluded, I suggest this reframe:

You've felt for a long time that there was something wrong with you. And if there's something wrong with you, you can't show the world who you are, can you? Because if you show the world who you are, they'll see those parts of you that are not good enough. And if you don't show people who you are, it's impossible to connect with them, isn't it? But it makes sense why you had to hide; it makes sense why you couldn't show them who you are. Doesn't it?

How does it feel now?

Rejected

If you were rejected a lot, we can change the meaning of the memory. Try this reframe:

If you can't show someone who you are, then you have to show them a mask. But what is the mask but a person you're pretending to be who you think they'll like. If that's the case, and it probably was, nobody really rejected you—they were rejecting the person you were pretending to be.

If you were rejected for who you weren't in the past, you can be accepted for who you are—in the present and in the future.

Masked

If you felt like you had to create a false persona around other people, think of it this way:

If you were putting on a mask and were accepted, then people gave you what they thought the mask persona wanted and needed. Not what *you* actually wanted or needed. Which means even if you were accepted, you didn't get what you needed in life.

When you drop the mask, you open up endless possibilities to get what you want and need. Because while you're wearing a mask and you wear it right, when people *do* try to treat you right, they are offering that to the person you're pretending to be. Which means that even if you're surrounded by good, smart people, you will not get what *you* really want and need. Ouch.

Unprotected

If you felt like you couldn't protect yourself at one time or another in life, consider this:
> If you think about fighters like Mike Tyson or Conor McGregor, you get that those guys can protect themselves. They're the guys who can handle themselves no matter what. But every time they step into the ring, they get the snot kicked out of them. Even when they *win*, they're walking away bloody and bruised. But that's the thing—they know enough to be able to protect themselves from the bad shots. They know how to *survive* that environment. Even if they get hurt, they know how to minimize the damage so that they can keep going. And that's what you've been doing all along, isn't it? Taking care of yourself as best you could, minimizing the damage so that you can survive, protecting yourself just like the best in the world.

Yes. That's exactly it.

Unsafe and Risky

Some of you may be so averse to pain and negative emotions that you won't pursue anything with any risk. Let me walk you through something dramatic—a skydiving example.
> Jumping out of a plane at fourteen thousand feet is 100 percent lethal. But hundreds of people do it every day. Because if you have a parachute, you'll be just fine. But the chute can malfunction, so you need to know how to fix it. And

you need a spare in case the original can't be fixed. You also need to know how to handle the whole contraption if you get stuck in a powerline or in a tree. Even when you land, you need to know how to tuck and roll so that you don't get hurt. Skydiving is *not safe*, but if you know the risks and mitigate them correctly with training and equipment, it is *safe enough*. It's safe enough to get that reward—the indescribable thrill of flying through the sky all on your own. It's never about risk. It's always about risk versus reward, skydiving or otherwise. And if you can manage the risk to where it's survivable, then you can go after those amazing rewards.

Surviving a situation is a win, in and of itself. Learning how to protect yourself by enduring a time when you felt unprotected—that, too, is a win. Facing rejection, being excluded, and feeling different—making it out through all of those are wins. *You* are a winner for having made it out alive. Winners are survivors; survivors win.

Whatever you had to do—fight, flee, freeze, fawn, or flop—you did. And so here you are. All were viable tools to ensure your exit from the situation. Even curling up into the human fetal position—an ultrabasic flop response—is a win if it helps you survive a situation.

A win is a win.

And you've won.

CHAPTER 6

YOU'RE SAFE NOW

Let me ask you a question.
Is there a part of your mind that, for any reason, feels like there's something wrong with you?

Most of you reading this are thinking, *No, I don't think so. You got me.*

But some of you are hesitating. Wondering. Ruminating. *You know, Ryan, if you really knew . . . If you just knew . . .*

That's OK. You might have a specific concern or uncertainty or doubt we haven't gotten to yet.

Your unconscious mind has been holding you back for a long time, trying to make sure you never end up in a dark place (or end up there again, if that happened before). We've established that you know the best way to ensure you never end up in that dark place: help yourself win.

Whatever may be causing that lingering hesitation, we're going to address it now.

Let me ask you another question. If you were able to go out in the world and start doing the things you wanted in order to succeed, would you feel like you were powerless and weak? Well, no. And if you did do those sorts of things, you would start getting more of what you wanted, wouldn't you? Would you feel like there's nothing wrong with you? Ha! Of course not. Because you would prove to yourself once and for all that you are capable, that you can get the things you want and need in life. You'd prove to yourself once and for all that you're not powerless and you're not weak; there's nothing wrong with you. If you proved all that to yourself, would there be any reason to go back to that dark place ever, *ever* again?

No. Never.

So think about this: Instead of having to protect yourself from going to that dark place—by holding yourself back and sabotaging yourself and so forth—you get another solution to keep yourself out of that space. Again, it's called winning. Proving to yourself the opposite of what you once believed, reinforcing the opposite of that, disproving those negative emotions, overturning those old unhelpful conclusions. All this is how you stay away from that dark place—beat that depression, despair, or suicidal ideation down. Stay away and keep away.

Let me walk you through a little exercise. This was originally pioneered by Mark Cunningham; he called it the Resource Organizer.[6] It goes like this:

> Remember a time when things didn't work right. It might even be the one on your mind since the beginning of this chapter. Got it? OK. Now place a frame around that memory. Adjust it a little so that all the colors of the picture become brighter, more intense . . . keep going . . . OK, more . . . very good . . . so bright till all the colors become one and you are staring at a blank white canvas.
>
> Now allow your unconscious mind to write, in words, the powerful, positive lesson it learned from that experience— the powerful, positive lesson that'll make sure that next time things go better, more the way you want them to, the way they should have gone all along.
>
> Give your unconscious mind all the time necessary over the next few seconds to go through however many words and

---

6 - See Mark Cunningham, "Renegade Hypnotist," https://renegadehypnotist.com/the-new-curriculum.

CHAPTER 6 - YOU'RE SAFE NOW

possibilities it needs. Instantly, easily, effortlessly, automatically, at the speed of thought or even faster, pulling out all those powerful, positive lessons. Helping make sure that next time, things go better, more the way you want them to go, the way they should have gone all along.

Now, in your mind's eye, turn around. Go on, literally turn around; look behind you. There you see hundreds upon thousands of those same white canvases with powerful, positive lessons written on each and every one. If ever you chose to look back at one sometime, the only thing you'll be able to see is that powerful, positive lesson. All the feelings of shame and guilt and insecurity, wanting to give up on life, being in the dark, cementing yourself emotionally, all that is gone, washed away, left behind. Because those negative thoughts and emotions hold no value to you anymore, do they? No. The only thing that matters is the powerful, positive lessons you've learned. Yes.

Turn around now. Face forward. You are now easily able to move through the world without shame, fear, guilt, hesitation, or reservation of any kind, effortlessly attracting people to you who understand and appreciate your best. You are establishing healthy boundaries and keeping toxic people out of your life.

Whenever you come across obstacles in your life, as one does, you just reach back to the powerful, positive lessons of the past. You reach out to your friends and mentors in real life and online, leveraging their powerful, positive lessons from all the things going wrong in their life and the ways they set them right. As a result, every obstacle falls; it goes over, under, around, or straight through, and you learn new, powerful, positive lessons along the way. You become stronger and more capable each and every time. You become wise and able to see the road ahead so much more clearly. Now any obstacles, any impediments, are learning opportunities. They're surmountable and able to be overcome using your own lessons and a little help from those you know you can trust. And then, one day, sooner than you ever thought possible, you become the man you want to be—strong, confident, able to do as he pleases. Living a life of success, love, connection, and abundance in every way. You see that clearly now, can't you? Yes. You do.

Now you are ready to help yourself win as much as humanly possible. You are ready to move through the world in a new way that makes the lessons of the past stick and stay. You are ready.

CHAPTER 7

MAKE YOUR EMOTIONS WORK FOR YOU

Let's quickly review how far we've come.

We have come to understand that there is nothing wrong with you. Because the challenges we all face are external, outside, impersonal. Thus, emotional signals received, once interpreted as pain and trauma and the like, are in fact *requests for help*. Nothing is wrong with you. Nothing *was* wrong with you either, those times and places that you used to think of with discomfort. No longer. Because you did the absolute best you could with the resources you had in order to survive. Which you did. It worked. You did the right thing. Every time. You are now. You could have made no better choice; *you already made exactly the right choice.*

Which furthermore means that your emotions have been here all along to help, not hurt, hinder, or hide. Your emotions are *not* working *against* you; removing the double negative, that means your emotions are here to serve you. We have alluded to this quite a bit throughout the book, covering how the mind works its way through emotional experiences to make sense of them, create meaning, learn lessons, and the like. But that exploration was entirely past-focused. What about future-paced? Is it possible to actively control or otherwise affect how your feelings . . . well, feel?

Obviously yes, as that is the purpose of this chapter! By far the most common emotion the people I work with want to create is the state of feeling valued. The result of this is unshakeable confidence at all times even in strange, unfamiliar, risky situations. Imagine: Confidence. Unshakeable. Every time.

To have such healthy self-esteem, you must believe yourself to be valuable. More accurately, you have to *feel* valuable. After all, you're not broken. Realize that something broken has less or no value at all. So any lingering negative emotions still stirring must mean that you're wounded or damaged—broken, not valuable. Not good!

This means we need to undo any remaining self-perception of emotional wound or unresolved trauma (the implication of those being that *I am damaged, therefore broken, therefore not valuable, therefore cannot have healthy self-esteem, and therefore do not have a life worth living*). You can understand how important this work is. It's so important that we've already touched on and expanded on it from chapter 1 onward. But it can't be an afterthought (or in this case, a forethought that is then forgotten). You cannot have healthy self-esteem if you fail to get this right. Any perceived emotional wounds *in the future* will thus equate to *I guess I'm still the problem after all*. No. Not good. Also not true. Lies limit. If you get wounded, if you get traumatized, there then needs to be things you must heal and fix. So you couldn't be good enough or ever deserving. It's not possible.

Let's talk about these emotions, of present and future. Because as we resolve them, we will be released to healthy self-esteem.

A helpful reminder: Everybody talks about emotions as if emotions are pain. Physical pain comes from a physical wound that's caused by a physical trauma—which is why everybody knows that emotional pain comes from an emotional wound that's caused by emotional trauma. Think about this: Put your hand on a hot stove. You yank your hand off, and your hand starts to hurt. What happened? Well, you didn't yank your hand off the stove because it was hurting. Your body realized the stove was hot and that it was gonna leave a mark. *I need to get my hand off there*, so your brain makes your body yank your hand off. It's too late. Now your body has a new problem. Your brain has already solved the first problem—hand on hot stove. But now it's got a new problem: Your hand is indeed burned, and you need to fix it. So it signals consciousness by sending pain. Pain is a signal that says, "Hey, look at this thing. There's a problem. It's broken. I need you to fix it." So, again, pain is a signal that says, "Look at something in particular because there's a problem; it's broken, and it needs to be fixed." Whether that's a burn on your hand, whether that's a broken leg, whether it's your nervous system going crazy because you've got fibromyalgia or you had a terrible accident. Pain says, "Look here; there's a problem. I need you to fix it."

This might feel like a little refresher course, but stay with me; we're about to reach a new synthesis.

Refusing to feel emotional pain and the inability to feel physical pain are connected. Imagine how badly someone who resists the signals of physical pain will hurt themselves. It's the same with emotional pain and the refusal to experience it. Yet emotions are a little different because they have two components: The first is the *meaning* of that emotion your mind is trying to convey—the signal it is trying to convey. The second is your *physiological* response to that signal. If you feel angry and you're getting all pumped up, that's your body preparing to fight and respond to the angry emotion that was triggered. If you feel fear and your hands get clammy, if you feel that nervousness and your stomach drops, that's your body preparing to run in response to that fear signal.

Every physiological response you feel in response to an emotion that's coming up is your body preparing to take action of some kind or trying to take action of some kind. There's an idea in Tantra that emotions are energy in motion. So the physiological response is your body trying to take action in response to that emotional cue. But this is important: if your body is taking action in response to a cue, if your body is trying to prepare to fight, trying to prepare to run, trying to hide, whatever that is, that's not pain.

Nothing's broken. Nothing needs to be fixed. That's your body responding appropriately and taking action appropriately in response to that mental signal of the emotion. That's not pain; that's not what that means.

It's not possible to make a decision without emotion.[7] But if we describe and talk about and define emotions and believe that emotions are pain, then we feel that strong emotion and we look where that emotion is being felt to find the problem. Because that emotion is being felt inside, the natural conclusion is that there must be something wrong inside me that I need to fix; there must be something broken inside me that I need to fix.

That's where that trap gets laid. Because feeling that intense emotion has us looking at ourselves as the problem that needs to be fixed. But that's not what's happening. Again, emotions are a signal from your unconscious mind to consciousness of how it's interpreting the *outside world* and what it wants you to do in response. The way it works is this: It shows you a picture from your unconscious mind to consciousness, and it gives you an emotion. The picture is what you're perceiving at that moment. Usually you're looking at the world right around you. Sometimes it's a memory and you're reexperiencing a moment in time. But almost always you're looking at the world outside you; you're not looking at you. You're not in the picture; you're not where the problem is that your mind is trying to solve. *There's a problem in the scene that I'm showing you.* The emotion is your signal as to which problem it's facing, which problem it needs to solve. And to that scene, you get five possible responses—five ways to respond to it that keep you alive.

---

7 - "The Interplay of Emotion and Reason," in *Neuroscience*, 2nd ed., edited by Dale Purves, George J. Augustine, David Fitzpatrick, Lawrence C. Katz, Anthony-Samuel LaMantia, James O. McNamara, and S. Mark Williams (Sunderland, MA: Sinauer Associates, 2001), www.ncbi.nlm.nih.gov/books/NBK10822.

Your Five Survival Responses (And How to Hack Them)

When we perceive a threat to our survival, we have five survival responses to draw on:

1. Fight
2. Flight
3. Freeze
4. Fawn
5. Flop

The *fight* response often triggers anger. Anger tells us that there's a problem and that we can make it go away by using force. This can be physical force, emotional violence, or psychological pressure. When someone crosses your boundaries and you get angry, your fight response can make you escalate emotionally or physically.

When it comes to your chances for survival, fighting is usually your best bet. If someone's trying to kill you and you can kill them first, the threat is resolved. That's why your first response is to fight (if you can).

If fighting doesn't work, or if fighting isn't an option, the next response is *flight*—run away from the problem as fast as you can. Flight triggers fear. Something out there is a threat, but if you try to fight it, you'll lose. If we can't make the threat go away, fear tells us to get away from it.

The third survival response is *freeze*, the hiding response. This anticipatory response happens when your mind notices a threat coming, but it's not here yet. In this case, your best bet is to freeze and hide so that it doesn't find you. Freeze triggers anxiety, the emotion associated with dealing with a potential threat in the future.

The fourth survival response is *fawn*. This is surrendering (or begging), which triggers desperation. You tried to fight, or run away, or hide, but you failed. Now you're left to beg the threat, *Please don't hurt me.*

The fifth and final survival response (which you've probably never heard talked about) is *flop*. Flop tells us we can't fight, run away, hide, or beg. What's left? Curl up in a ball with your hands over your head and pray to God that the threat stops before you're dead. This triggers the emotion of depression. You've run out of options, and the only thing you can do is lie down and take it. You can't fight it. You can't avoid it. You can't hide from it. You can't beg your way out of it. All you can do is take it.

All that said, the proper response to feeling *any* of these emotions is to get curious. If you're angry, you should figure out what the problem is and what you can do to leverage force of some kind to make it go away. If you're feeling afraid, what are you afraid of? How do you get away from it? I'm feeling anxious. OK, what's the problem coming up? How do I avoid it? OK, so I need to beg. What the hell do I need to say to make this stop? What's going to shut them up and make this quit?

Two More . . .

The next two emotions to cover are also survival-level issues, but they're not responses to an existential threat. The next emotion is sadness. Sadness is an emotion that says you've lost something valuable; you've lost something that is needed for survival. You have probably felt this emotion at some point in your life. Probably at many points.

The response here is, again, to get curious. If you've lost something valuable, what did you get instead? What lessons did you learn? What positive things can you take from that experience? What can you salvage from that situation?

The difference between an Irish wake and a funeral is this: At a funeral, you're mourning the loss of somebody. At a wake, you're celebrating their life. You're keeping the good memories and cherishing them and sharing them.

The latter of the two nonthreat response emotions is regret. Regret is like sadness, but instead of losing something valuable, there's an opportunity to gain something valuable . . . and you screw it up. So then the question is, again, getting curious: How did I mess it up? What could I have done instead? What lessons have I learned? What benefits did I get?

When you're feeling any of these seven emotions, that emotional state is your unconscious mind asking your conscicusness for help solving the problem. It's asking for permission, for more information, for . . . something, anything, to make it better. But because the problem may be a survival-level threat, your unconscious minc cannot take no for an answer (we've established by now why this is the case). This is where coercion comes in.

Unconscious Coercion: The Three Archetypes

I've asked you to do something for me. You told me no, and I'm going to make you do it anyway because I need it. That's coercion.

The first coercive archetype is the *bully*. The bully says, "I'm going to apply pressure until you do what I ask you to do." Whether that's physical force, threats of violence, social pressure, psychological pressure, emotional pressure, financial pressure, or whatever it happens to be.

The way your unconscious mind acts when it's asking your consciousness for help is this: If you feel an emotion and ignore it, what does it do? It cranks up the volume, increases the pressure, and intensifies the signal until you respond. It tries to *bully* you into taking action. It can't take no for an answer. So it cranks up the intensity of the emotion. It screams louder. You're still not listening? It screams even louder.

There's a threshold of force beyond what you can't push, where the intensity of the emotion becomes a threat in and of itself. This is where interpreting negative emotions—pain—comes in. *Oh my God, I'm too sad. I can't stand to feel that. I gotta turn that down.* But the problem is, if you are suppressing, ignoring, or evading your emotions, you are telling your unconscious mind, *Not only can I not help you solve that problem but also being in this situation is painful enough that I can't take it.* So now your unconscious mind

1. doesn't have a solution for navigating that situation or problem, and
2. it has to keep you away from being in that situation or confronting that problem again because you can't handle it.

Because these are survival-level issues that are being addressed, that situation is now a threat to your survival. So now your life gets narrower and narrower and narrower as more and more experiences become off-limits.

The second coercive archetype is the *victim*. The victim says, "I've got a problem, you've got a solution. You've told me no, so I'm gonna make you feel bad until you help me." The victim revels in guilt and shame.

Guilt is an emotion that says, "I've got a problem, you've got a solution, and you're not giving it to me."

There are a few important things to recognize with guilt. First, *they* have a problem, you don't, and they're trying to make *their* problem *your* problem, which means they don't care about you. Second, even if *you* have a solution, it's up to *you*. It's entirely *your* choice as to whether you give it to them or not, whatever it is that's being asked for or demanded. That's your free choice. If they're not giving you an option, if they're trying to coerce you again, they don't care about you. It becomes a situation where you look at it and consider, *OK, they* have a problem; I have a solution. Do I want to give it to them or not? Is it appropriate? Is it going to cause me more trouble than it's worth? Will they even be grateful? Are they just going to keep on coming? Will they keep making things harder and harder for me? By looking at guilt through the lens of somebody trying to make their problem your problem so that you feel badly enough to solve it for them, you increase your agency.

With the victim archetype, shame joins guilt. Shame is quite simple. Shame is an emotion that says, "You failed to meet the standard. You didn't measure up."

An appropriate response to shame is—once again—to get curious. Is that a reasonable standard to which you should be held or to which you should hold yourself? If you're feeling ashamed that you haven't gone to the gym, then OK, you failed to go to the gym. You said you were going to, but you didn't go. Is there a reason that you should hold yourself to that standard or not? Well, if you're a bodybuilder, that's important. If you're not a bodybuilder, maybe it's OK to miss a day or two. If you're sick, maybe it's not OK to be holding yourself to the standard of going to the gym every day. But if it's an appropriate standard, then the next question is, *How do I meet that standard? What am I doing wrong? How do I need to fix it?* This is a healthy response and effectively counteracts the shame. So really, shame can be a useful tool because it gives you discernment on what you should and should not be held to standard wise.

Shame comes into play on all matters of ego. *I gotta be a good man, I gotta be a good father, I gotta be a productive citizen*, so forth and so on. Others may be leveraging those against you, or you might be leveraging all that against yourself.

This is the source of one of the biggest problems, one of the biggest impediments to doing this work, and that is self-loathing. This is where you have a conscious set of standards, and by not being able to be or do that thing, you judge yourself harshly. You start hating yourself and saying, *I'm the problem. I'm the reason I cannot meet these standards. I'm the reason I'm unacceptable to myself.* The important point here is that you've created a *conscious* standard for yourself. It's not an *unconscious* one; consciousness has turned against the rest of the self.

And again, the way to get a handle on it is through rational self-correction: Is this realistic to expect? If so, what can I do now? If not, what is? And so forth and so on.

The last unconscious coercive archetype is the trickiest, and that is the *seducer*. The seducer says, "I asked you to do something, and you told me no. Fair enough. But if you change your answer, if you say yes, I'll give you a cookie. I'll make you feel good. I'll reward you in some way." This is insidious because it makes you feel pleasure. This is what traps all the entrepreneurial, high-performance types. You feel good when you're pursuing your goals. The unconscious mind uses that feel-goodness as a tool to make you run from your pain. *Keep on chasing these goals, keep on chasing these goals. Feels good, feels good, feels good. Got your goal? Great. Make another one. Keep running.* It's like the carrot on the stick that's dangled in front of you while you're running endlessly. That can be as much of a trap as any of the negative emotions are.

Now that we've reviewed the seven emotional responses and the three coercive archetypes that our unconscious can use to intensify those emotions to trigger survival-seeking action, what do we find?

Well, we find ourselves coming full circle a bit, don't we? We again see that emotions are not pain; they are specific signals that are asking you to help with certain problems. That means that if it's not pain, then it doesn't come from an emotional wound. And if you don't have an emotional wound, then it wasn't caused by an emotional trauma, correct? This means something interesting; it means you've never suffered a trauma in your entire life. If emotions are not pain, then they don't come from emotional wounds. If there are no emotional wounds, then there is nothing to heal.

CHAPTER 7 - MAKE YOUR EMOTIONS WORK FOR YOU

So any "trauma" from the past is now reframed as simply a situation where you were not able to figure out a way to win. You were in a tough situation, didn't have any options, and couldn't find a way out, so your mind cranked up the emotion because it begged for an answer, and you didn't have one. Trauma is an event in somebody's life when they could not find a solution to the problem at hand, and their mind freaked out and made them feel intense, negative emotion at the same time. That's it. It was just a time when you couldn't figure out how to win.

This is why the flop response is so important. If you fight the thing off, it's not a problem. You don't get hurt. If you flee successfully, it can't find you, it can't hurt you, so you don't get hurt. Both of those are ways to win. Both of those mean you don't get hurt. Both of those mean you don't suffer. By talking about survival in terms of avoiding being hurt, anytime you are hurt, that's a threat to survival. Which means that anytime you *do* feel significant emotional pain, significant negative emotion, you're still considering it to be a negative, to be pain. That, again, is a threat to survival. But flop is a highly effective survival strategy. Curl up in a ball, take your beating until they knock it off, and you get up and walk away. Being able to endure and simply keep breathing, simply surviving, is a win. Is it a clean win? No. Do you get hurt? Yes. Are you still breathing? Yes. That's technically a win in the way that counts.

We have to reinforce that message because you are now able to experience pain, negative emotion, without making it a survival issue, without making it something you have to avoid. Now it becomes something you can engage with. And that opens up the list of options you have in your life—*massively*. You don't have to run from emotional pain. Because emotions aren't pain. Negative emotions are signals; negative emotions are your mind asking for help solving a problem. The best part is that it's telling you what problem it needs to solve.

Problems are not hard to solve on their own. Once you figure out what the problem is, it's easy to fix.

Here's another key takeaway from this helpful little rabbit hole of reminders: Every emotion you experience is simply your own interpretation of the events and the world around you and how your unconscious mind wanted you to respond. It's your interpretation, which means nobody made you feel anything. The negative emotions you experienced were not caused by someone else, which means they're under your control—then, now, and forever.

Which also means that nobody else can make you feel anything you don't want to feel. Nobody can push your buttons the way they used to be able to do because you know what those are (the archetypes of coercion that your own unconscious tries to use on you). Now that you know them, you are immune to them.

There's nothing wrong with you, and there never was.

CHAPTER 8

HOW TO FEEL VALUABLE

I struggled with Asperger's for years, and I did so in silence. No one understood me—or I them. Not as a child, not as an adult. It was brutal. The world felt cruel. So brutal and cruel that I often found myself seeking a reason to live—as an adult *and* as a child. Eventually, I realized that I could suffer forever, or I could, as a little boy would reason, be Batman. Not Bruce Wayne but Batman. His life kind of sucks. He sacrifices himself for others. That's better than suffering forever.

This brought me to understand something about the nature of sacrifice: Throwing trash away doesn't hurt. Sacrificing yourself—throwing yourself away—that hurts. Therefore, there must be inherent value. My life *must* have value, I realized. Anything sacrificed must have inherent value. I had been sacrificing myself through my intelligence career and in my close personal relationships, giving without expecting to receive reciprocally in return, whether that be love and affection or recognition and requisite reward. Working in counterterrorism and in the intelligence community and realizing that the number of bad guys never decreased—and also that the system of US foreign policy did nothing productive with the space we worked to create for them, as in Iraq, Afghanistan, both complete and total shitshows—yeah, that was tough. Nevertheless, sacrifice is how I realized I had value. That and trash.

So then I wondered, *If my life has value, how much value?* I began to calculate my value based on my salary, my socioeconomic status, and the attractiveness of my significant other. Yet all these were externally run numbers. Justifying my inherent value as a human by what society thought.

There came a point when I realized I didn't need to justify my existence to anyone anymore. I could choose to live. For me. Which meant I no longer had to make excuses to anyone for being me—*for being Batman*. I was able to make that choice *after* I realized I could pursue what I wanted in life, which is what we cover in chapter 9. For now, we circle the concept and meaning of value.

This is not new. Back in caveman days, our likelihood of surviving was based on our capacity to perform physical labor. Are we smart enough and strong enough and fast enough to chase down and kill the wooly mammoth? If yes, we get to eat; otherwise, we starve and die. (So the question of *my* survival was a question of how much work *I* could do.)

After a while, we humans developed agriculture, but survival was still dependent on how much physical labor we could do. Eventually we reached capitalism. These days, nobody goes and gets what they need to survive. I don't build my own house, make my own clothes, or hunt down my own food. Nobody does that. We all go to a job, get this stupid thing called money, and trade it for what we need to survive. Which means these days in the modern West and in the world at large, survival is not about our capacity to do physical labor. Everything we need to survive is based on an exchange of value. Now the question our mind has to answer is not *How much work can I do?* It's *How valuable am I? How valuable am I as a human being, as a person?* Because how much I'm worth tells me how much value I can exchange for the things I need to survive and the things I want in life. You can look at it as how many dollars you have in the bank in terms of self-worth determining what you can buy.

CHAPTER 8 - HOW TO FEEL VALUABLE

What you can buy is what we call deservedness. *Do I deserve the yacht? Do I deserve the supercar? Do I deserve a supermodel girlfriend? Do I have enough points in the bank? Am I masculine enough to afford a supermodel girlfriend? Do I deserve it?* And whether I "deserve" these is entirely based on how much worth I have, how valuable I am.

So what's the problem? Well, if there are issues with yourself that you need to fix, then you're broken. Are broken things particularly valuable? No, broken things are not valuable, and we know that. As long as you think there's something wrong with you, so long as there's something you need to fix about yourself, then you cannot be valuable enough, because you know you're broken.

But by this point, we've come to recognize that there's nothing wrong with you and there never was. There's nothing to heal and there never was, which means you're not broken, which means for the first time in your life, you can be valuable. You can be good enough. We have to figure out how to measure the value of a person. There is no universally accepted definition of the value of a person.

"Oh, it's what you do in the world." Does that mean that babies have no value? Because they can't do anything in the world. "Oh, well, based on potential then." What about the high infant mortality risk throughout most of human history? Babies don't have any value, then, if most had no potential productivity that would go unrealized, sadly. So that's not a good answer. "Well, men are supposed to be strong." Great. So how much of a bench press do I, as a man, need to do to be a man? And is it my bench press, or am I deadlifting? What if I'm quadriplegic? Can I not be a man?

You start doing this a little bit and you realize every definition of value we have is arbitrary. The way we measure the value of a human life is also arbitrary. That makes sense because if you feel like you're not good enough, you want to find a way that you can measure up. You look around for the things you can do, for something you're good at, and say, "I'm going to measure my value that way." But you're doing that on a rational, logical basis, not on an emotional, instinctive-mind basis. The thing is, feelings don't care about facts. If you're angry about something, it doesn't matter what the facts are. Nobody has ever won an argument with their wife saying, "Honey, there's no reason to feel that way, to be that upset. You're blowing it out of proportion." That never works. Which means the emotional truth of a situation isn't reliant on the facts. Ever.

You can never prove wrong feelings like "I'm not good enough." If the thing you're measuring is arbitrary, and the way you're measuring it is also arbitrary, then you can come up with any answer you want based on what you choose to measure and how you choose to measure it. If I choose to measure my value based on how strong I am and I'm a gymnast, maybe I measure it by how long I can hold an iron cross. If I'm a bodybuilder or a powerlifter, I'm measuring it on my deadlift. If I'm Dr. Jordan Peterson, I'm not doing it on my bench press or my iron cross; I'm doing it based on how morally strong I am.

You can get whatever answer you want by changing the question—the thing you decide is the measure of value and how to measure it. Which means that your value as a person is just a choice. It's an arbitrary choice even, being made on an unconscious level, not made based on any external factor. You're not proving it from the outset; it doesn't work that way. You've already decided what your value is and it's arbitrary. It's just a choice.

Everybody out there trying to prove to themselves how strong they are and how good they are and how much they measure up are trying to disprove the feeling, to disprove the conclusion that's already been drawn, which doesn't work.

Checking back in with ourselves now, we're in an interesting place: It's possible, finally, to have value. It's possible to be good enough because you're not broken anymore. There's nothing to fix,

CHAPTER 5 - HOW TO FEEL VALUABLE

nothing to heal. Now you have a choice: You get to choose whatever value you want to rate yourself by. How valuable do you choose to be?

"Well, I'm gonna be infinitely valuable!" you might say.

Welcome to the trap. If you're still trying to set a value, then you're still measuring. And if you're still measuring, it's possible the answer is *still* not enough—or it doesn't feel that way, at least. You may have high value, sure, but do you have high enough value to get everything right? If you're still counting how many points you have in the bank to figure out what you can buy, it may well be that you don't have enough to buy whatever you're wanting. Because the reason you want to know how valuable you are is because you want to know what you deserve.

But how many points you need to buy something, how expensive something is in terms of personal value to get it, is also arbitrary. There's no Sears catalog of life. You can't look it up on Amazon.com. That number doesn't exist.

That number's also completely arbitrary, and you're the one who made it up. Again, it's your choice; it's your choice how valuable you are. But it's not your choice how valuable you need to be to deserve anything in particular. If the number of points you have is completely arbitrary and just a choice, and the points you need to deserve something are completely arbitrary and just a choice, why the hell would you bother trying to measure that in the first place?

Why would you design a system where it's possible for you to fail? Why would you design it in such a way that it's possible for you to not be good enough? That's dumb. Don't do that. The way out of the trap, as I see it, is this: *I have decided that I'm good enough.*

I spent most of my life feeling like I wasn't good enough. Which begged the question, of course, "Good enough for what?"

I'm good enough to deserve whatever I choose. Do I deserve that? Yes. To have enough points? Yes. Why? Because I'm good enough. How many points do I have? I've got enough. Why? Because I'm good enough. *Why? Because I freakin' chose to. It's my choice. I made it. I'm good enough to deserve it. What about that? Do I deserve that? Yes. Am I good enough for that? Yes.*

You simply make this the new default. You know the choice, the answer to those questions. Just default it to yes and leave it there. *Am I good enough? Yes. Do I deserve it? Yes. End.*

This makes things interesting because the unconscious mind judges true and false based on whether things match what it already believes. Recall that beliefs are assertions that are true without evidence, even despite evidence to the contrary. If an old belief was "I'm not good enough," then it didn't matter how much the person tried to succeed; they never measured up. Effort is never enough.

But if you set your personal value and deservedness to *yes*, if the answer is "I'm good enough," if the belief is "I'm good enough and I deserve whatever I choose," then no number of external events can prove that wrong. It doesn't matter what happens in life, whatever tragedy befalls, whatever comes along. Because it doesn't change your value as a person; it doesn't change what you deserve.

I happen to know, understand, and believe this personally. Last year (from the time of this writing), I had a psychotic break. An actual one. Not "ha ha, life's hard. I had a really bad weekend, lol, lmao." No. I mean an acute manic episode. I literally went insane over the course of a week and a half. As a result, I got arrested. Indecent exposure misdemeanor, felonious assault against a police officer, two more misdemeanors for resisting arrest and transport, multiple days in jail, then $36,000 in bail, and $25,000 in legal fees, fines, and lawyer services. My girlfriend had already left me, and my business collapsed. (Try to picture in your mind what, exactly, happened with those few details, and the scene is . . . yeah. It was. It really was.)

That series of unfortunate events breaks most who suffer them. And yet I was able to keep on trucking. Why? Because what transpired did not change my value. It was not a reflection on me as a person. It was something that happened, something I had to deal with. It's a problem to solve—no more and no less. It didn't change what I deserve.

What happens once you make that choice to believe "I decide that I'm good enough to deserve whatever I choose"? Nobody and nothing can change that belief—not even you. It's just default. For the rest of your life. You don't have to do anything to earn it. You don't have to do anything to deserve something. You just deserve it. You're just good enough. That's the truth from that point on—nothing wrong with you, nothing to heal, nothing broken, nothing to fix. You're good enough. You deserve whatever you choose. Nothing can change that. The fact that I have Asperger's syndrome, the fact that I have ADHD, the fact that I have bipolar disorder, the fact that I literally went mad and "ruined" my life for a brief season . . . none of that means my mind is broken. It means that my brain is wired in a rather inconvenient way, which I've always known. My design is just different from most people's—the vast majority of people's—and as a result, I've got several challenges when it comes to navigating life.

I've stopped trying to have an ego identity or a conscious identity. I'm not trying to be an entrepreneur. I'm not trying to be an alpha male. None of that matters. I'm not trying to define myself from the outside anymore. I'm simply a being who is doing things in the world. Every bit of self-esteem and self-value is based on inside-out, not outside-in.

That makes you resilient. Which makes things interesting for what comes next.

Think of work as your capacity to endure suffering, which is like physical pain. Your capacity to do physical work is based on your capacity to suffer physically. Well, if emotions are no longer painful, then you can't suffer *emotionally*. That's not pain. What happens is, to do the work to bring something into your life that you want, you must solve a series of problems. That's all you're doing. You're trucking along . . . solving problems, solving problems, solving problems.

And either you're solving the problem in front of you, or you're hitting a wall and don't know which problem to solve first or how, at which point you start getting emotional signals, which is your mind asking for help to solve the as yet unsolved. All you must do then is get curious, find the problem behind the problem, solve it, solve the anterior problem, and you're back and running again.

Because negative emotions are not pain nor are they something to avoid. You can be in that negative emotion as long as needed to figure out what the problem is so that you can solve it. Which means your capacity to solve problems is basically infinite. If it's possible for your mind to figure it out, either alone or in conjunction with other people, you'll figure it out—as long as you listen, pay attention, and stay curious.

Thus, success becomes inevitable. Because there's nothing to stop you from solving problems. There's nothing holding you back. *You deserve it. You've chosen to go get it. You can solve problems.* You know how to listen to your mind when it's telling you what problem it's looking for. You know how to ask for help. And you know *who* to ask based on what problem you're trying to solve because of how you feel. The feeling is the way.

Let me pull back the veil on all this a little more. In hypnosis, we tell your mind how to process reality. Pain control hypnosis, for example, is telling your mind to interpret those signals from your body differently. Instead of feeling pain, you feel discomfort or heat. Here's how. Remember the instinctive mind, the emotional mind, and the rational mind? Here you're giving them different functions, different jobs. Your instinctive mind is in charge of physical survival. Your rational, logical mind is in charge of external world, verifiable facts. And your emotional mind is responsible for values and meaning. Instead of your emotional mind having to send all those emotional signals to consciousness to get help, now the rest of your mind, your instinctive mind and your intellectual, rational mind, knows what

CHAPTER 8 - HOW TO FEEL VALUABLE

your emotional mind needs from them whenever you hit a particular problem-solving wall. Instead of having to bring that emotional content up to the boss—up to consciousness—your emotional mind can simply ask for help from the other parts of your mind and from your unconscious mind. Those other parts of your unconscious mind know automatically how to help solve the problems it's facing.

In short, your unconscious mind now works together so efficiently that it doesn't need any help from the conscious mind at all—until and unless it's reached its capacity to solve the problem on its own. You've also made it so that your unconscious mind cannot coerce and force your consciousness into doing anything. Which means that now consciousness is truly in charge again, as the ultimate decider. So your life gets zen and easy, fast. It gets frictionless. You've taught your mind how to work together with itself as an integrated, well-oiled, well-trained team. You've given effective standard operating procedures for problem-solving so that it can get information from the other parts of the unconscious mind that it needs to, without bothering you. Now your consciousness is free to do what it does best: planning for the future.

Should I do this, or should I not do this? Do I want to do this, or do I not want to do this? Because where I want to be in five years is . . .

That's the job of consciousness. Long-term planning. Being the ultimate decider. Acting as the witness of your life as it plays out.

What you want is inevitable.

CHAPTER 9

WHAT YOU WANT IS INEVITABLE

Consider this.

Deserving and *having* are two different states. Because you deserve something doesn't mean you actually get to have it. Having something depends on doing the work to go get it. But remember, we've changed the question our mind asks. From "Do I deserve the thing?" to "Am I willing to do the work to go get the thing?" Now survival is no longer based on "Do I have enough value to exchange?" It's "Am I willing to do the things necessary to bring that into my life?" That's a much easier question to answer; it's a much easier set of problems to solve.

Who sets your value? I ask clients this. I also ask them, "Who decides what you deserve?" Ultimately, the only answer to both becomes *you*. Even if it's been someone else, it's you who decides to accept that external rating of worth. Even so, it's you who decides your value and you who sets your worth.

Back to deserve versus have and who decides both. In the West, especially from where I write in the United States, we've got the Protestant work ethic. There's this core belief that what you have is what you deserve. Furthermore, what you have is a reflection of God's favor. From the Protestant perspective, you can tell how much God loves you and how righteous you are based on what you have. Which is what drives that Protestant work ethic. *I bust my ass and I'm favored by God, and then I get a bunch of stuff, proving I'm favored by God.*

The problem is that having and deserving are two different things. I could deserve love and affection and not be able to have it. If I'm walking around in the middle of the desert, I probably deserve to get a glass of water and survive, but there's no guarantee that's going to happen for me.

This distinction is critical because we're all trying to figure out how deserving we are based on what's available in our respective environments. Let's get extreme to break the usual frame. If a four-year-old gets leukemia, does that mean they deserve leukemia? If a different child crossing the street gets hit by a car, do they deserve to get hit by the car? Jeffrey Epstein deserved to have all that money because that's what he had, right? So that means he deserved it.

OK, you get it. *Deserving* cannot mean *having* always or even mostly. Otherwise we have to draw conclusions that are uncomfortable. Let's deal with the *having* side. To have something, you work to attain it. And in your capacity, that's solving a series of problems. I need to solve a series of problems to get a Lamborghini, for example; I have to earn that money.

Your capacity to do work to solve problems is based on your capacity to suffer—your capacity to withstand pain. You work until you get sore and you can't work anymore. That's your threshold. The longer you can ignore that pain, the greater you let the pain grow, the more work you can do. This is part of what makes Navy SEALs so effective, by the way—they're willing to withstand immense amounts of physical suffering. This means their capacity to achieve is so much greater.

Most of the things we're doing to get what we want in life, the work we're doing, isn't physical work. It's mental. Your capacity for mental work is your capacity to endure mental and emotional suffering. So when you were defining emotions as pain, as states of being

CHAPTER 9 - WHAT YOU WANT IS INEVITABLE

to avoid, that belief massively limited your capacity to do hard mental work. If I'm feeling ashamed, guilty, insecure, so forth and so on, those are pain, which means my body has to run away from it. My mind has to run away from it, too. This limits the space that I can work in mentally and thus the amount of work that I can do. Making sense?

All this is to say: Your emotions are a guide to the solution. You follow your pain, you follow the emotional signal, you get curious about what that could be, all of which leads you in a certain direction. Then, *boom*. You identify what the problem is that your mind's trying to solve, and you start crunching away on the real problem. Once you know what that is, it's straightforward to fix.

Your capacity for mental and emotional work now becomes infinite because you either know the problem you're supposed to be solving, you're actively working on it, making progress, or you're feeling something, getting some clue from your emotional mind telling you, *This isn't it*, and you get curious about alternatives. You go down a different pathway to figure it out. Once you figure it out—you overcome that obstacle or overcome that wall—you're back on track again.

By *not* avoiding negative emotions, by listening to the negative emotions, by welcoming the negative emotions, you're giving your mind a way to signal that you need to change course, that you need to be looking at something else, that you need to be doing things differently. That's incredibly useful. Which means that your ability to have the things you want increases massively. It no longer becomes a question of "Do I deserve this?" It becomes a question of "Am I willing to do the work?"

That work just got a heck of a lot easier.

From now onward, you have complete and total access to your mental and emotional faculties. No more survival mode, baby. Your mood is not a threat to your existence anymore. You disarm the suicide time bomb, the self-deletion time bomb, so that now your mind doesn't have to protect you from yourself anymore, which means now you are not at war with your emotional state. The only things that become a threat to survival are things that *are* a threat to your survival. The only times you drop into survival mode are when things are going to hell in a handbasket, when everything's chaotic, when there are *actual* problems you need to solve, which massively lowers your stress level.

This has a few different implications. The first is that when you're in survival mode, you never get the chance to rest, relax, and recover. Because you're always under threat. "It's always something." There's always some chaos or disorder you have to respond to, some threat you have to mitigate or attack back. So you never get the chance to let down your guard. Finally.

The second implication is this: If you're not in survival mode all the time, not everything's an emergency and you don't have to treat it as such or worry about whether tomorrow's coming. You have time. You have all the time in the world, which means nothing has to be done right now unless it *has* to be done right now. You get to take your foot off the gas for once. You can go with things at a measured pace. You can focus on doing the right thing at the right time instead of forcing yourself to be productive, forcing yourself to be efficient, waiting for the right time to make things happen. It gives you ease. It allows you to move through the world in a completely different way and much more efficiently.

Because you start doing the right thing for the right reasons, at the right time, and in the right way, you don't have to do a quick, sloppy job. Instead of trying to succeed because you're attempting to overcome your insecurities, which is like doing the right thing for the wrong reason, you start wanting to succeed. You're wanting to do a project because of the impact it would have—or simply for the joy of creation.

CHAPTER 9 - WHAT YOU WANT IS INEVITABLE

To sum up, everybody's stuck in survival mode because they're trying to manage their emotional state. Their emotional state is a threat to their existence, and they have to manage it. Until you get to a place where you don't have to manage your emotional state anymore, until you get to a place where you're not operating on fear or pain or needing to prove yourself, you're stuck in survival mode. Everything has to be done right now. Everything's an emergency. As soon as you fix that, then you're not in survival mode anymore. You're not trying to survive your emotional state. You're allowed to slow down. You're allowed to do things at a much more deliberate pace. Now you have all the time in the world to get things done.

CHAPTER 10

NOW THAT EVERYTHING HAS CHANGED

With this book, we've given each level of your mind a specific area of responsibility, and we've taught it how to give the other parts what they need. This means that your consciousness doesn't have to get involved mediating conflicts nearly as often. It also means that training the rest of your mind how to work together smoothly allows you to finally be at peace. To finally get to stop fighting yourself. Here's why.

In every high-performing organization, responsibility and decision-making are pushed down to the lowest level possible because that's the information environment most qualified to make that decision, to shoulder that responsibility, and to do both well. The CEO should not be deciding for the graphic design team what color to use on the *About* page of the website. That's the designers' purview.

Similarly, your consciousness should not be involved in resolving the conflicts between your rational and emotional minds. And indeed, now that you've done this work, that is no longer necessary. This is true for two important reasons:

1. By giving your rational and emotional minds specific areas of responsibility, your unconscious mind now knows which to listen to in which circumstance.
2. Now that we've defined what emotions mean and what your mind needs from you in those situations, your mind can automatically gather that information from your emotional mind, your rational mind, and your environment without needing to bombard your consciousness with unnecessary emotional content.

If the consciousness is the CEO of your mind, the CEO does only CEO work: long-term planning, strategy, and so on. If the CEO's not doing that, they should be out golfing. Why? Because they have people to handle everything else.

This is what I mean by *Winner Peace*. Your mind can sit back, relax, and watch with certainty and authority as things unfold without being distracted by unnecessary thoughts and emotions. This frees you up to reevaluate how things are going, how you want them to go, and what's needed to make that happen.

Wants versus Needs: A New Perspective

Your motivations are changing. You're going to need to take another look at your life and what you're doing and why—start looking at the reasons behind what you were doing.

Which brings us to *wants* versus *needs*. What we want is usually based on what we believe we needed in the past but didn't get. This is not always obvious. The goals we create are in many ways designed to fix a problem of the past. For example, many internet marketers-turned-entrepreneurs believe they need to hit a freedom number. This is usually the monthly recurring revenue, often postexpenses,

CHAPTER 10 - NOW THAT EVERYTHING HAS CHANGED

posttax, that they need to feel free. Or something. And it's *feel*, not *be*. Many of them are living in communities that are not the highest cost of living in the world. Their mortgage (or rent) is less than $2,000 per month. What the hell do they need $100,000 per month, every month, for? Why want that? It's usually because when they were in their early twenties, or even as children (or both), they needed something they could not afford. *Need*. Like a nonclunker, reliable car. Perhaps there was a traumatic event when Dad's car wouldn't start, and he lost his job because he couldn't go to work. That unfulfilled need, witnessed during formative years, becomes a semi-irrational want in adulthood. It's rational to want to be able to provide for your family and to do so well. The irrationality is that $100,000 every month is a made-up number. It feels even, clean, and like it will *more than provide for every single need you could possibly imagine*. It's totally arbitrary.

But what happens when you do the work? *This* work, which you've read about in this book? What happens is that things change dramatically. You understand that the lack when you were young was not your failure and did not mean anything about you as a person—or your father. This means that you don't have to correct (or overcorrect) for those feelings of inadequacy by setting your sights on made-up, arbitrary, over-the-top goals.

Finally, you get to *want* your *needs*. By that I mean you get to *really want* your *actual needs*. Going back to the earlier example, that means the need to cover living expenses and then some, possibly even to pay the mortgage off early.

Which means figuring out what those are and engineering for them instead. Consider the famous Scott Adams advice to pursue systems over goals. In this context, that means a system to meet your needs. Or *systems*, plural. Building systems to meet your needs rather than your wants is the best way to navigate life, after you've changed.

A Few Words on Free Will

Before you did this work, your mind had taken away your free will. It trapped you in the cage or left you on the treadmill. But now that you no longer need your mind to protect you from yourself, something very interesting has happened: you now have a choice.

Up until this point, you did not have a choice about being on or off the treadmill or in or out of the cage. You couldn't stop what you were doing, meaning it was a compulsion, not a choice. Now that you don't have to protect yourself from yourself—you don't have to run or hide—you can choose any path you want for any reason you want. It becomes equally acceptable to build a multimillion-dollar business or to decide to move to Bali and spend the rest of your days drinking beer and surfing. Previously, your mind might have attempted to manage up goals and dreams like these, convincing you not to pursue them or coercing you out of them through shame. Your mind knows its place now. You have your free will back. Which means you have a very important choice to make: What game do you want to play? There are more than one.

The Games We Play

Remember the game that cannot be won? You're in a situation where you don't make the rules. But they keep changing anyway. The goal moves, too. It's rigged from the start. It's not possible to win, and that's not your fault. So don't. Don't even play. Play different games. You've already realized you can. This is what the entrepreneurial journey is all about. Once you realize you can play your own game by your own rules, you will find a game that you can win. Maybe that's entrepreneurship. Or art. Or athletics. Something you have a unique talent for. So you go all in. You base your self-esteem and self-worth

CHAPTER 10 - NOW THAT EVERYTHING HAS CHANGED

on measurable outcomes, almost like you're turning life into a video game and trying to run up a high score.

The problem with playing that game is there are winners and losers. And most importantly, in the age of the internet, you can always find someone who is playing that game better than you. You don't stop comparing yourself to other people; you just change the other people you're comparing yourself to—people who are more successful, more creative, more athletic—just *more*—than you. They're winning; you're losing.

Simon Sinek, the best-selling author of *Start with Why* fame,[8] has often said that there are two types of games: finite games and infinite games. Finite games have a set number of players. They have tight rules. There's a way to keep score to ensure that there are clear winners and obvious losers.

Finite games are attractive. Entrepreneurs love to play them. That's all they often do. They're trying to compete on profit margin, return on ad spend, and the other typical key performance indicators to measure business success. Influencers on social media want to prove themselves by increasing follower count and audience engagement rate.

Why do we play finite games? Simple. We're trying to prove to ourselves that we're good enough, and we deeply fear we might not be. Yes, the game can be won, but it can always be lost. Put another way, there are ways to win, but there are other ways for other people to win way more than you, and thus you are a loser relative to them. OK, so you made $1 million last year? Someone ten years younger than you in a second world country but in the same industry (and with a handicapped wife plus nine kids at home) earned $10 million doing exactly what you do—and worked half as many hours. It's extreme but it's not. There is always someone winning the finite game and thus someone else losing.

---

8 - Simon Sinek, *Start with Why: How Great Leaders Inspire Everyone to Take Action* (New York: Portfolio, 2009).

What happens when you don't need to prove anything to yourself anymore? What happens when your base belief is *I am good enough. I do deserve whatever I choose. There's nothing wrong with me, and there's nothing to heal.*

Interestingly enough, the first thing that happens is you stop having to prove to yourself that you're good enough. That you deserve it. Because you only have to prove things that you *don't* believe. If you believe in God, for instance, you don't have to do anything to prove it. You just believe. If you believe the earth is flat, I mean . . . good luck. You won't be inclined to try proving it because you just *know*.

Notice how beliefs persist and will even ignore evidence to the contrary. That's the nature of belief; it's something that is true to you without evidence and despite evidence to the contrary. But we keep trying to prove those things wrong; we only try to prove things wrong that we believe or that we want to believe differently. If we believe we're not good enough, we want to prove that wrong. That's when we try to get proof. That's when we look for the closest finite game we can and start playing.

In *V for Vendetta*, the protagonist played by Hugo Weaving says, "Beneath this mask is an idea, and ideas are bulletproof." Beliefs are bulletproof, too, because beliefs interpret all the input from the outside world through the lens of *Does this match what I already believe?* If it matches, it's considered true; it gets accepted. If it doesn't, it's false by definition and gets ignored, which means you can't prove a belief wrong. It's just not possible.

Which means that once you believe there's nothing wrong with you, when you believe that you're good enough, there's nothing to heal, and you deserve what you want in life, nothing can prove all that wrong. No external circumstance can change that. *You can't even challenge those beliefs on your own!* You are now bulletproof. Success is inevitable.

CHAPTER 10 - NOW THAT EVERYTHING HAS CHANGED

This is important. Why is it important? You probably figured it out. All of a sudden, all the things you were doing to prove to yourself that you're good enough to win a finite game, all those pursuits you had, with all that extrinsic motivation, they change. Which means that your goals change, too, because now you're all about doing the right thing for the right reason. You don't have to use reason to prove to yourself that you're good enough, nor do you have to run from your pain or your fear because that's what was driving the vast majority of life up until this point—up until you read this book and everything changed.

Until you're ready to start playing infinite games. Infinite games do not have set players. Players come and go. They do not have set rules. The rules change. There's no way to keep score, and there are no winners and losers. But the goal of an infinite game is to keep playing. Life is an infinite game. People come in and out of your life all the time. You're playing the game by different rules with each individual person.

The beautiful reality of playing life as an infinite game is that you can't lose because there's no score; there are no winner or losers. You cannot lose that game.

In an old *Calvin and Hobbes* comic, the characters are playing Calvin Ball. There they are out playing the game, running around, having a grand old time. As soon as somebody got an advantage and started winning, they changed the rules. Why? To keep it interesting, to keep the game going. They would just swap back and forth, changing rules, depending on what they could come up with on the fly. And so the real game became this: How creative can you be about creating new rules? How fun can you make it? How interesting can you make it?

My own compass these days is, *What is it that I can do that's interesting and fun?* And the rest just takes care of itself. I'll meet somebody new and wonder what game I can play with this person. I start asking questions, and if we're having fun, great. If not, thank you for playing. Then go find somebody else to play Calvin Ball with.

We go from a game that cannot be won, to a game that can be won or lost, to an infinite game you cannot lose. Many people are a little anxious over this. It's understandable. Many had relied on their pain and fear for so long to drive them. It felt like legitimate pain and fear because they were using dirty fuel to get things done. But the idea that you're just going to quit life and abandon your responsibilities and become a monk . . . no. Flat-out ridiculous. You chose that particular endeavor for a reason (you know exactly what I'm talking about), even if it was a finite game. But there's something inherently rewarding about what you're doing already. Isn't there? For me, for example, I built www.ryanthehypnotist.com into a real business. I started doing this work because I wanted to help people. Sure, I make decent money. It's not even hard. I'm basically working part-time for the equivalent pay of multiple full-time jobs.

What generally happens now and in the immediate short-term future is that your motivations for the things you're doing shift. Instead of doing it out of pain, you're doing it out of intrigue, challenging yourself because you find it interesting, you find it fun, you find it important.

Even two years ago my goal was to build a multimillion-dollar business. Today my *system* is that which ends human suffering. That's a better goal. Bigger and better.

You don't need to play the hustle-and-grind game anymore. The world does not need another . . . whatever it is you thought you were supposed to be in order to be acceptable. You don't have to prove anything to yourself anymore. It's OK. And so that opens up the aperture to consider much more interesting endeavors.

One of the greatest shifts this book has already made for you is that we've taken you from an external locus of control to an internal locus of control where your worth and value are no longer judged by someone else. They're not dependent on external factors at all. We've taken your reality back for you; we've placed *who you believe you are* inside you and locked that truth away where no one else can get to or touch it. Which means you no longer have to prove anything to anybody else. You don't need to work hard anymore. At anything.

And yet . . . you do. It becomes easier to work hard. But more so *smart*. That's what comes easy now. The guy who can work smart is going to outcompete the one who is just working hard, ironically. Because the guy who works smart knows when it's time to flip the switch and grind. He knows when it's time to push the pedal to the metal. But he knows that he doesn't have to do that if it's not appropriate for the moment. Again, doing the right thing for the right reason at the right time in the right way—this is what you do now.

You have confidence; you *are* confidence. People often confuse confidence with competence, which is more foreknowledge that you will deploy your skills in an upcoming situation at or above expectations. That's competence. You may be *competence*, yes, and now you are *confidence* as well.

I'll admit, this trips some people up right at the finish line. If a guy is already perfect at being himself, and by definition he is, why then is he not confident? Well, that goes back to the ego construct versus the subconscious construct of self. You have an idea of who you want to be and you're not that yet, so you don't feel confident in yourself. But watch this: If you're running off an internal locus of control over that subconscious concept of self, if you let the ego go—which is what happens when you do this work—now, all of a sudden, you feel 100 percent competent at being you. Because there's nothing wrong with you, what's not to like? Uh, nothing. Exactly. Now that you've done this work, you're in an interesting place—you can accept who you are. Who you are is good enough. You're perfectly fine, which means it's OK to be who you are. You don't have to create a persona to show the world. You just get to be you.

All alone with your thoughts is a good place now. You become zen, fast. Because unless there is some problem that cannot be solved by your unconscious mind, there's no reason to bring it to your consciousness. When things do bubble up into conscious awareness, it's usually not yelling at you because it knows you're listening. The intensity of negative emotions becomes less now, which means the amount of maintenance you need to sustain that levelheaded calm baseline mood is pretty much none. As long as you're handling business the way you should, of course—and anybody reading this book is a highly capable individual who can do that. It's all being handled. So you get to save joy and pride for the times when you're freakin' doing something good. You cannot get stuck in the pleasure trap again. Which also means you don't have to spend a half an hour a day meditating to clear your mind. Your mind is clear when you wake up in the morning. You don't have to spend all that time doing cold plunges or whatever to crank up your dopamine just to quiet the voices in your head. They're not yelling anymore. There's not a problem anymore. Life becomes easy and chill. And all that puts you in a place where you can do the appropriate amount of work with the appropriate amount of effort at the appropriate time rather than forcing yourself to hustle and grind, pursuing goals and trying to rank up and get a high score to make yourself feel better.

No more. You are you, and you are more than enough. You can start playing games other people can't conceive of. You can stop worrying about quarterly revenue goals and start worrying about actual impact. You can shift from millions of dollars to millions of people. I wrote earlier how I changed from wanting to own a seven-figure business to wanting to end human suffering. The reason Elon Musk bought Twitter was not to turn it profitable; it was to save freedom of speech for the entire world. He's building rockets to save the human race—and yes, to make some money along the way.

What kind of unbelievable impact could you make on the world when you stop trying to compete in finite games?

The Next Step

You're probably wondering about this. You might be wondering where to go from here.
Ready to go on an adventure?
I'll explain.
The people I work with are high performers universally and biohackers usually. Interest in change is guaranteed. Awareness of and even use of alternative therapies: ketamine, mushrooms, and more. Psychedelics do help create resets. They are phenomenal provocation and discovery tools. They take you on a journey of your choosing. But there's no control or direction. The ride takes you where it takes you. It shows you the most important thing for you to see at that moment.
It can be helpful to use these to find a target for more guided discovery and resolution, like hypnosis. This integration work, being incredibly hard, can be assisted by other modalities (not replaced by them). If you want to know what to work on next, consider learning more about psychedelics and hypnosis.
There is a free chapter on exactly this available at www.ryanthehypnotist.com/bonus so that you can learn more.

ACKNOWLEDGMENTS

Every book has an author, and every author has a loosely organized lifelong team of inspiration. Some of those key people on my team have included Sarah Clark, Shabnam Rajah, and Ether Arkon. This trio collectively helped save my life—thank you. My journey was to make life worth living, then live that life. Because of you three, together with more than a dozen other coaches and experts like you, I now pass on the gifts I've received. This book would not exist without you, and I might not anymore either. Thank you.

www.ingramcontent.com/pod-product-compliance
Lightning Source LLC
Chambersburg PA
CBHW030656060526
44119CB00097B/454/J